"Herminia Ibarra's insightful new book is an inspirational read for everyone who has a passion for leading and developing people. In times of rapid change, her profound research and hands-on approach of 'transforming by doing' is broadening horizons."

—JOE KAESER, CEO, Siemens AG

"In this provocative new book, Herminia Ibarra challenges conventional thinking on leadership. She takes into account the high-velocity, shape-shifting context that we all live in and offers an action-oriented, practical playbook on leadership, identity, and change. It is a must-read for the contemporary leader."

—SUSAN P. PETERS, Senior Vice President, Human Resources, GE

"Herminia Ibarra has created a valuable and successful model for helping forward-thinking professionals move up the corporate ladder. She has created a vivid road map for achieving career growth based on 'learn while doing.' I'd encourage every professional looking to get to the next level to read this book!"

—MARSHALL GOLDSMITH, author, *New York Times* and global best seller *What Got You Here Won't Get You There*

"Based on Herminia Ibarra's extensive research and experience working with executives, *Act Like a Leader, Think Like a Leader* provides insightful and practical advice about how to do the hardest thing of all—change ourselves. By acting, as opposed to thinking, we can all become better leaders."

—LINDA A. HILL, Wallace Brett Donham Professor of Business Administration, Harvard Business School; coauthor, *Being the Boss: The 3 Imperatives for Becoming a Great Leader*

"In order to be a better leader, you need to 'act first, then think.' Read this book to find out what a most original thinker, Herminia Ibarra, has in mind."

—CHARLOTTE BEERS, former CEO, Ogilvy & Mather;
former Under Secretary for Public Diplomacy and Public Affairs,
US Department of State

"In today's increasingly volatile and uncertain world, leadership is more important than ever. But new skills are required. This intelligent and thought-provoking book is for those who really want to make a difference—those willing to act their way into leadership situations they might previously have thought themselves out of."

—PAUL POLMAN, CEO, Unilever

"Herminia Ibarra clears the myths about leadership with her fresh, profound, yet down-to-earth book about the importance of action over introspection. She's the perfect coach, showing aspiring leaders how to get over themselves and see the world around them. Her stories and tools make this a must-read for blossoming as a leader."

—ROSABETH MOSS KANTER, Harvard Business School Professor;
best-selling author, *Confidence* and *SuperCorp*

Act Like a Leader, Think Like a Leader turns the leadership development paradigm on its head and makes a compelling argument that one becomes a better leader through 'outsight' as opposed to insight."

—BETH AXELROD, Senior Vice President, Human Resources,
eBay Inc.

"Modern business requires us to lead differently, yet conventional approaches to gaining new leadership skills have proven less than effective. Fortunately, in *Act Like a Leader, Think Like a*

Leader, Herminia Ibarra provides us with a wonderfully practical way of taking control of our own leadership transformation."

—TIM BROWN, CEO, IDEO; author, *Change by Design*

"Herminia Ibarra reverses the polarity of how we understand and practice leadership. The result is a powerful, compelling, and practical call to arms for all leaders. Leaders and would-be leaders alike should read this book and take action."

—STUART CRAINER, cofounder, Thinkers50

"An unprecedented combination of globalization, demographics, and depleted pipelines is generating a dramatic shortage of qualified leaders. This will be a unique chance for those who rise to the occasion by redefining their work, their networks, and their identity. Ibarra's extraordinary book is the best resource I can recommend to capture this opportunity for any professional who wants to become a leader, survive as such, and grow into a much greater one."

—CLAUDIO FERNÁNDEZ-ARÁOZ, Senior Adviser, Egon Zehnder;
author, *It's Not the How or the What but the Who*

"From the world's foremost authority on identity at work comes this must-read call to action that will accelerate your leadership development in all parts of your life. Ibarra powerfully demonstrates how 'outsight' trumps insight for producing sustainable personal growth and provides practical, easy-to-follow lessons on how to use it."

—STEWART D. FRIEDMAN, best-selling author, *Leading the Life You Want* and *Total Leadership*

"With vivid examples and thought-provoking research, Ibarra takes future leaders beyond the normal platitudes to a deeper and richer understanding of what it is to become a better leader. Her action-orientated approach, profound understanding of networks, and wisdom about identity deliver a book that will change the way we think about the transition to leadership."

—LYNDA GRATTON, Professor of Management Practice, London Business School

"Leadership is the most elusive and difficult attribute to pinpoint, but Ibarra nails it with a pragmatic 'Do' attitude. Her research-based approach is refreshing and a must-read for newly minted as well as long-in-the-tooth leaders."

—JEFFREY A. JOERRES, Executive Chairman, ManpowerGroup

"Ibarra will help leaders develop their actions before their thoughts, which is the best way to learn. Her real-world approach is refreshing and valuable."

—DAVID KENNY, CEO, The Weather Company

"Anyone—quite possibly everyone—can be a leader in the #SocialEra. Not because you have the right title or look the part but because you know how to lead ideas—and do what is in this book. *Act Like a Leader, Think Like a Leader* is a smart, counter-intuitive guide to stepping up to leadership through action, not introspection."

—NILOFER MERCHANT, best-selling author, *The New How* and *11 Rules for Creating Value in the #SocialEra*

"I love this book. It focuses on the 'work' the best leaders do to get a little bit better every day. *Act Like a Leader, Think Like a Leader* is a practical and useful collection of ideas for becoming more effective as a leader."

—SANDY OGG, Operating Partner, Blackstone

"Have you had it with navel-gazing? In this terrific book, Herminia Ibarra offers the antidote. She reframes the leader's quest as a process of looking outward, rather than inward, for direction, development, and opportunity. Her conclusions—her 'outsights'—come from careful observation and current research and include smart, practical suggestions for expanding your leadership opportunities."

—DANIEL H. PINK, best-selling author, *To Sell Is Human* and *Drive: The Surprising Truth About What Motivates Us*

"The world is changing fast, and with it the expectations about how many and what kind of people need to transition into leadership. Herminia Ibarra's new book helps these individuals expand their jobs, make their contributions more strategic, diversify their networks to connect with all stakeholders, and become playful with a sense of purpose."

—GILBERT PROBST, Managing Director, Leadership Office and Academic Affairs, World Economic Forum

"Defying conventional wisdom, Herminia Ibarra moves beyond the mantra of merely building on one's traditional strengths and demonstrates the need for personal transformation and growth based on real-life experiences. Given the magnitude of today's challenges and the huge impact of leadership on the future of our economies and societies, this 'call to action' for leaders should be widely heard and will greatly enhance the practice of leadership."

—RICHARD STRAUB, President, Peter Drucker Society Europe

ACT LIKE A LEADER, THINK LIKE A LEADER

ACT LIKE
A LEADER,
THINK LIKE
A LEADER

HERMINIA IBARRA

Harvard Business Review Press

Boston, Massachusetts

The web addresses referenced in this book were live and correct at the time of the book's publication but may be subject to change.

Library of Congress Cataloging-in-Publication Data
Ibarra, Herminia, 1961–
    Act like a leader, think like a leader / Herminia Ibarra.
      pages cm
    ISBN 978-1-4221-8412-7 (hardback)
1. Leadership. 2. Executive ability. 3. Organizational change. I. Title.
    HD57.7.I35 2015
    658.4'092–dc23

                        2014033424

The paper used in this publication meets the requirements of the American National Standard for Permanence of Paper for Publications and Documents in Libraries and Archives Z39.48-1992.

ISBN: 9781422184127
eISBN: 9781422184134

For Hector and
my parents

Contents

Thinking is for doing.

—S.T. Fiske

How can I know what I think until I see what I do?

—adapted from Karl Weick

ACT LIKE A LEADER, THINK LIKE A LEADER

The "Outsight" Principle: How to Act and Think Like a Leader

'M LIKE THE FIRE PATROL," says Jacob, a thirty-five-year-old production manager for a midsized European food manufacturer. "I run from one corner to the other to fix things, just to keep producing."[1] To step up to a bigger leadership role in his organization, Jacob knows he needs to get out from under all the operational details that are keeping him from thinking about important strategic issues his unit faces. He should be focused on issues such as how best to continue to expand the business, how to increase cross-enterprise collaboration, and how to anticipate the fast-changing market. His solution? He tries to set aside two hours of uninterrupted thinking time every day. As you might expect, this tactic isn't working.

Perhaps you, like Jacob, are feeling the frustration of having too much on your plate and not enough time to reflect on how your business is changing and how to become a better leader. It's all too easy to fall hostage to the urgent over the important. But you face an even bigger challenge in stepping up to play a leadership role: you can only learn what you need to know about your job and about yourself by *doing* it—not by just *thinking* about it.

Why the Conventional Wisdom Won't Get You Very Far

Most traditional leadership training or coaching aims to change the way you think, asking you to reflect on who you are and who you'd like to become. Indeed, introspection and self-reflection have become the holy grail of leadership development. Increase your self-awareness first. Know who you are. Define your leadership purpose and authentic self, and these insights will guide your leadership journey. There is an entire leadership cottage industry based on this idea, with thousands of books, programs, and courses designed to help you find your leadership style, be an authentic leader, and play from your leadership strengths while working on your weaknesses.[2]

If you've tried these sorts of methods, then you know just how limited they are. They can greatly help you identify your current strengths and leadership style. But as we'll see, your current way of thinking about your job and yourself is exactly what's keeping you from stepping up. You'll need to change your mind-set, and there's only one way to do that: by acting differently.

Aristotle observed that people become virtuous by acting virtuous: if you do good, you'll be good.[3] His insight has been confirmed in a wealth of social psychology research showing that people change their minds by first changing their behavior.[4] Simply put, change happens from the outside in, not from the inside out (figure 1-1). As management guru Richard Pascale puts it, "Adults are more likely to act their way into a new way of thinking than to think their way into a new way of acting."[5]

So it is with leadership. Research on how adults learn shows that the logical sequence—think, then act—is actually reversed in personal change processes such as those involved in becoming a better leader. Paradoxically, we only increase our self-knowledge *in the process of making changes.*[6] We try something

FIGURE 1-1

Becoming a leader: the traditional sequence (think, then act) versus the way it really works (act, then think)

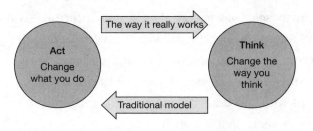

new and then observe the results—how it feels to us, how others around us react—and only later reflect on and perhaps internalize what our experience taught us. In other words, we act like a leader and then think like a leader (thus the title of the book).

How Leaders Really Become Leaders

Throughout my entire career as a researcher, an author, an educator, and an adviser, I have examined how people navigate important transitions at work. I have written numerous *Harvard Business Review* articles on leadership and career transitions (along with *Working Identity*, a book on the same topic). Interestingly, most of what I've learned about transitions goes against conventional wisdom.

The fallacy of changing from the inside out persists because of the way leadership is traditionally studied. Researchers all too often identify high-performing leaders, innovative leaders, or authentic leaders and then set out to study who these leaders are or what they do. Inevitably, the researchers discover that effective leaders are highly self-aware, purpose-driven, and authentic. But with little insight on how the leaders became that way, the research falls short of providing realistic guidance for our own personal journeys.

My research focuses instead on the development of a leader's identity—how people come to see and define themselves as leaders.[7] I have found that people become leaders by doing leadership work. Doing leadership work sparks two important, inter-related processes, one external and one internal. The external process is about developing a reputation for leadership potential or competency; it can dramatically change how we see ourselves. The internal process concerns the evolution of our own internal motivations and self-definition; it doesn't happen in a vacuum but rather in our relationships with others.

When we act like a leader by proposing new ideas, making contributions outside our area of expertise, or connecting people and resources to a worthwhile goal (to cite just a few examples), people see us behaving as leaders and confirm as much. The social recognition and the reputation that develop over time with repeated demonstrations of leadership create conditions for what psychologists call *internalizing* a leadership identity—coming to see oneself as a leader and seizing more and more opportunities to behave accordingly. As a person's capacity for leadership grows, so too does the likelihood of receiving endorsement from all corners of the organization by, for example, being given a bigger job. And the cycle continues.

This cycle of acting like a leader and then thinking like a leader—of change from the outside in—creates what I call *outsight*.

The Outsight Principle

For Jacob and many of the other people whose stories form the basis for this book, deep-seated ways of thinking keep us from making—or sticking to—the behavioral adjustments necessary for leadership. How we think—what we notice, believe to be the truth, prioritize, and value—directly affects what we do. In fact, inside-out thinking can actually impede change.

Our mind-sets are very difficult to change because changing requires experience in what we are least apt to do. Without the benefit of an outside-in approach to change, our self-conceptions and therefore our habitual patterns of thought and action are rigidly fenced in by the past. No one pigeonholes us better than we ourselves do. The paradox of change is that the only way to alter the way we think is by doing the very things our habitual thinking keeps us from doing.

This *outsight principle* is the core idea of this book. The principle holds that the only way to think like a leader is to first act: to plunge yourself into new projects and activities, interact with very different kinds of people, and experiment with unfamiliar ways of getting things done. Those freshly challenging experiences and their outcomes will transform the habitual actions and thoughts that currently define your limits. In times of transition and uncertainty, thinking and introspection should *follow* action and experimentation—not vice versa. New experiences not only change how you think—your perspective on what is important and worth doing—but also change who you become. They help you let go of old sources of self-esteem, old goals, and old habits, not just because the old ways no longer fit the situation at hand but because you have discovered new purposes and more relevant and valuable things to do.

Outsight, much more than reflection, lets you reshape your image of what you can do and what is worth doing. Who you are as a leader is not the starting point on your development journey, but rather the outcome of learning about yourself. This knowledge can only come about when you do new things and work with new and different people. You don't unearth your true self; it emerges from what you do.

But we get stuck when we try to approach change the other way around, from the inside out. Contrary to popular opinion, too much introspection anchors us in the past and amplifies our blinders, shielding us from discovering our leadership potential and leaving us unprepared for fundamental shifts in the situations around us (table 1-1). This is akin to looking for the lost

TABLE 1-1

The difference between insight and outsight

Insight	Outsight
• Internal knowledge	• External knowledge
• Past experience	• New experience
• Thinking	• Acting

watch under the proverbial streetlamp when the answers to new problems demand greater outsight—the fresh, external perspective we get when we do different things. The great social psychologist Karl Weick put it very succinctly: "How can I know who I am until I see what I do?"[8]

Lost in Transition

To help put this idea of outsight into perspective, let's return to Jacob, the production manager of a food manufacturer. After a private investor bought out his company, Jacob's first priority was to guide one of his operations through a major upgrade of the manufacturing process. But with the constant firefighting and cross-functional conflicts at the factories, he had little time to think about important strategic issues like how to best continue expanding the business.

Jacob attributed his thus-far stellar results to his hands-on and demanding style. But after a devastating 360-degree feedback report, he became painfully aware that his direct reports were tired of his constant micromanagement (and bad temper) and that his boss expected him to collaborate more, and fight less, with his peers in the other disciplines, and that he was often the last to know about the future initiatives his company was considering.

Although Jacob's job title had not changed since the buyout, what was now expected of him had changed by quite a bit. Jacob had come into the role with an established track record of turning around factories, one at a time. Now he was managing two, and the second plant was not only twice as large as any he had ever managed, but also in a different location from the first. And although he had enjoyed a strong intracompany network and staff groups with whom to toss around new ideas and keep abreast of new developments, he now found himself on his own. A distant boss and few peers in his geographic region meant he had no one with whom to exchange ideas about increasing cost efficiencies and modernizing the plants.

Despite the scathing evaluation from his team, an escalating fight with his counterpart in sales, and being obviously out of the loop at leadership team meetings, Jacob just worked harder doing more of the same. He was proud of his rigor and hands-on approach to factory management.

Jacob's predicaments are typical. He was tired of putting out fires and having to approve and follow up on nearly every move his people made, and he knew that they wanted more space. He wanted instead to concentrate on the more strategic issues facing him, but it seemed that every time he sat down to think, he was interrupted by a new problem the team wanted him to solve. Jacob attributed their passivity to the top-down culture instilled by his predecessor, but failed to see that he himself was not stepping up to a do-it-yourself leadership transition.

The Do-It-Yourself Transition: Why Outsight Is More Important Than Ever

A promotion or new job assignment used to mean that the time had come to adjust or even reinvent your leadership. Today more than ever, major transitions do not come neatly labeled with a new job title or formal move. Subtle (and not-so-subtle) shifts in your business environments create new—but not always clearly articulated—expectations for what and how you deliver. This kind

FIGURE 1-2

How managers' jobs are changing, from 2011 to 2013

The percentage of respondents saying these are the responsibilities that have changed over the past two years

Different stakeholders to manage
56%

Increase in cross-functional responsibilities
53%

Significant change in your business environment
49%

Increase in multinational scope of the job
42%

30% or more increase in number of people reporting to you
41%

Shift to one or more new functions
40%

30% or more increase in your P&L
30%

Start-up of a new business or market
22%

Source: Author's survey of 173 INSEAD executive program alumni, conducted in October 2013.

of ambiguity about the timing of the transition was the case for Jacob. Figure 1-2, prepared from a 2013 survey of my executive program alumni, shows how managerial jobs have changed between 2011 and 2013.

The changes in managerial responsibilities are not trivial and require commensurate adjustment. Yet among the people who reported major changes in what was expected of them, only 47 percent had been promoted in the two years preceding the survey. The rest were nevertheless expected to step up to a significantly bigger leadership role while still sitting in the same jobs and holding the same titles, like Jacob. This need to step up to leadership with little specific outside recognition or guidance is what I call the *do-it-yourself transition*.

No matter how long you have been doing your current job and how far you might be from a next formal role or assignment, this do-it-yourself environment means that today, more than ever, what made you successful so far can easily keep you from succeeding in the future. The pace of change is ever faster, and agility is at a premium. Most people understand the importance of agility: in the same survey of executive program alumni, fully 79 percent agreed that "what got you here won't get you there."[9] But people still find it hard to reinvent themselves, because what they are being asked to do clashes with how they think about their jobs and how they think about themselves.

The more your current situation tilts toward a do-it-yourself environment, the more outsight you need to make the transition (see the sidebar "Self-Assessment: Is Your Work Environment Telling You It's Time to Change?" at the end of this chapter). If you don't create new opportunities within the confines of your "day job," they may never come your way.

How This Book Evolved

This book describes what outsight is and how to obtain it and use it to step up to a bigger leadership role, no matter what you're doing today. The ideas in this book are the same ones in The Leadership Transition, an executive education course that I developed and taught for over ten years at INSEAD. Nearly five hundred participants from over thirty countries have gone through the program. I have read their sponsors' evaluations, analyzed the participants' 360-degree feedback, listened to their challenges, and watched the evolution of their personal goals, from the time the leaders first arrive to when they return for a second round three months later. From the earliest days of teaching The Leadership Transition, my INSEAD colleagues and I have used the outsight ideas to guide participants successfully through their transitions.

Both this book and my course are based on my decades of research on work transitions. The notion of outsight that is central here originated in some of my earlier work on how professionals stepped up from project management to client advisory services and on how people change careers.[10] In both areas of study, I found that introspection didn't help people figure out how to do a completely different job or move into a completely different career—or even figure out if they wanted to. This finding also held for people stepping up to leadership.

Many of the ideas about how to increase outsight also came out of my original research. For example, my PhD thesis on why some people's ideas for innovative products and processes meet fertile ground, and why other ideas don't, led to some leadership-networking concepts discussed here.[11]

As my leadership course evolved, I zoomed in on two cohorts for more in-depth interviews. A research assistant and I interviewed the thirty participants in one year's program—all the participants from different companies and industries. We also wrote case studies about a few participants; the case studies are the basis for some of the stories you will read in this book. Years later, we interviewed a second cohort, a group of forty high-potential managers striving to move up to the next level in a large consumer-goods company; we hoped to flesh out the pitfalls and successful strategies involved in stepping up.

I also took advantage of many opportunities to validate or adapt my theories about what it takes to step up to bigger leadership roles. I shared my findings with dozens of companies and many alumni and HR and talent management groups. I spoke with headhunters about the alarmingly high failure rates of the executives they placed, and I met with leadership development specialists trying to put in place better practices in their companies.

FIGURE 1-3

The outsight principle: becoming a leader, from the outside in

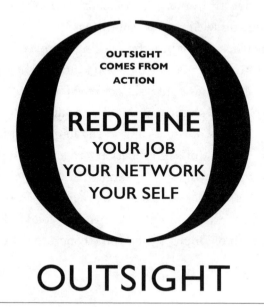

I adapted my course accordingly, in light of all these inputs. In 2013, I conducted a survey of my alumni to learn more about how their jobs were changing, what leadership competencies the leaders thought were necessary, what was helping them to step up, and what they still found hard. The result is this book about outsight and how we can increase our outsight to become better leaders.

How Outsight Works

The stepping-up guidelines detailed in this book are based on three critical sources of outsight. First is the kind of work you do. Second, new roles and activities put you in contact with new and different people who see the world differently than you do. Rethinking yourself comes last in this framework, because you can only do so productively when you are challenged by new situations and informed by new inputs. Developing outsight is not a one-shot deal but an iterative process of testing old assumptions and experimenting with new possibilities.

So the best place to begin is by making changes in how you do your job, what kinds of relationships you form, and how you do what you do (figure 1-3). These outsight sources form a tripod, working together to define and shape your identity as a leader (or to hold you back). Ignore any one of the legs, and the foundation is not stable. That's why no amount of self-reflection can create change without important changes to what you do and with whom you do it.

How, specifically, do these outsight principles work? Let's examine each of the three essential sources of leadership outsight, using Jacob as an example, to see some concrete actions.

Redefine Your Job

As Jacob's intuition told him, stepping up to leadership implies, first and foremost, shifting how he spends his time. But two hours of quiet time in his office isn't the right investment. In fact, most of the required shifts in what Jacob does must take him off the factory floor, where his office is located.

In today's fast-paced business world, value is created much more collaboratively, outside the lines of self-contained groups and organizational boundaries.[12] People who can not only spot but also mobilize others around trends in a rapidly changing environment reap the greatest rewards—recognition, impact, and mobility. To be successful, Jacob must first redefine his job, shifting from a focus on improving current factory operations to understanding the firm's new environment and creating a shared strategic vision among his functional peers so that his manufacturing operation is better aligned with organizational-level priorities. The work involved in understanding how his industry is shifting, how his organization creates value, how value creation may change in the future, and how he can influence the people who are critical to creating value—whether or not they are inside his group or firm—is very different from the many functional activities that currently occupy his time.

As mentioned earlier, Jacob wanted to concentrate on the capital investments his company would require over the next two years, but he had no time for this sort of introspection. He complained about "the fire patrol" of overseeing his people and his production facilities. But he knew that his boss expected him to craft a strategy based on a view of the overall business as opposed to the perspective of a super–factory director and to actively work to bring on board the relevant stakeholders.

Jacob's focus so far had been successful and is typical of many managers at his stage of development. Early in our careers, we accomplish things within the confines of our specialty groups. We make the transition to managing the work of others, usually within our own functional or technical areas, typically in domains in which we are expert. But as we start to move into bigger leadership roles, the picture starts to change radically.[13] When I asked the participants in my survey what competencies were most critical to their leadership effectiveness, they listed competencies that required a great deal of outsight focus (figure 1-4). But not surprisingly, 57 percent of the same managers also responded "somewhat or very true" to the statement "I let the routine and operational aspects of my work consume too much of my time."

As psychologists remind us, knowing what we should be doing and actually doing it are two very different things.[14] Shifting from driving results ourselves to providing strategic direction for others is no easy task. It requires collaborating across organizational units or functions instead of mostly working within the confines of our own groups or functions. It means refocusing our attention from having good technical ideas to getting buy-in for those ideas from an extended and diverse set of stakeholders. Ultimately, we are

FIGURE 1-4

The most important leadership competencies

The percentage of respondents saying these leadership abilities are important or extremely important to being effective today

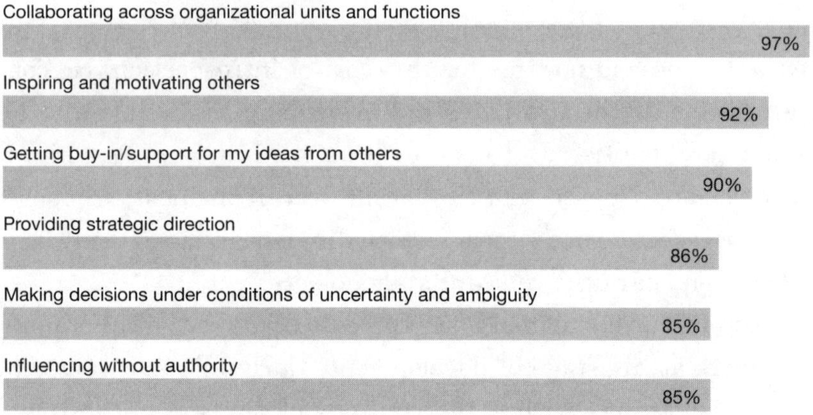

Collaborating across organizational units and functions

97%

Inspiring and motivating others

92%

Getting buy-in/support for my ideas from others

90%

Providing strategic direction

86%

Making decisions under conditions of uncertainty and ambiguity

85%

Influencing without authority

85%

Source: Author's survey of 173 INSEAD executive program alumni, conducted in October 2013.

moving away from implementing directives that are handed down from above to making decisions under conditions of uncertainty or ambiguity about how the business will evolve. All of these shifts depend on us to change our priorities and points of view about what matters most. Only then do we actually start changing the way we allocate our time. The only place to begin is by moving away from the comfort and urgency of the old daily routine.

Chapter 2 further develops the idea of redefining your job as the first step to increasing your outsight. It argues that the place to start stepping up to leadership is changing the scope of your "day job" away from the technical and operational demands that currently consume you in favor of more strategic concerns. Prioritizing activities that make you more attuned to your environment outside your group and firm, grabbing opportunities to work on projects outside your main area of expertise, expanding your professional contributions from the outside in, and maintaining slack in a relentless daily schedule will give you the outsight you need to think more like a leader.

Network Across and Out

It's hard to develop strategic foresight on the factory floor. As we saw, to step up to leadership, Jacob needed to see the big picture, to spend less time "on the dance floor" and more time "up on the balcony," as Harvard professor Ronald Heifetz describes it.[15] Jacob would thus also have to change the web of relationships within which he operates to spend more time outside.

Ultimately, he needed to understand that the most valuable role he could play would be a bridge or linchpin between the production environment and the rest of the organization. Like many successful managers, he had grown accustomed to getting things done through a reliable and extensive set of mostly internal working relationships; these had paid off handsomely over the years. For Jacob, these operational networks were very useful for exchanging job-related information, solving problems within his functional role, and finding good people to staff teams. But they stopped short of preparing him for the future, because they did not reach outside the walls of his current mind-set.

When challenged to think beyond their functional specialty and to concern themselves with strategic issues to support the overall business, many managers do not immediately grasp that these are also *relational*—and not just analytical—tasks. Nor do they easily understand that exchanges and interactions with a diverse array of current and potential stakeholders are not distractions from real work, but are actually at the heart of the managers' new roles.

But how do we come to think more cross-functionally and strategically? Where do we get the insight and confidence we need to make important decisions under conditions of uncertainty? As experienced leaders understand, lateral and vertical relationships with other functional and business unit managers—all people outside our immediate control—are a critical lifeline for figuring out how our contributions fit into the overall picture and how to sell our ideas, learn about relevant trends, and compete for re-sources. Only in relation to people doing these things do we come to understand and value what they do and why. These outsights help us to figure out what our own focus should be—and there-fore, which tasks we can delegate, which ones we can ignore and, which ones deserve our personal attention.

Our networks are critical for our leadership development for another reason, too. When it comes to learning how to do new things, we also need advice, feedback, and coaching from people who have been there and can help us grow, learn, and advance. We need people to recognize our efforts, to encourage and guide early steps, and to model the way. It helps a lot to have some points of reference when we are not sure where we are going.

But the sad state of affairs, however, is that most of the execu-tives I teach have networks composed of contacts primarily within their functions, units, and organizations—networks that help them do today's (or yesterday's) job but fail to help them step up to leadership. In Jacob's case, he was on his own to figure it out. Sim-ilarly, many of the people who come to my courses also report that they are not getting the help they need from inside their depart-ments and companies. My survey shows that the biggest sources of help were external. The managers' bosses or predecessors came in fourth place as bases of support, putting the managers squarely in a classic do-it-yourself transition (figure 1-5).

In fact, only 10 percent of the participants answered "very true" when asked if they had a mentor or sponsor who looked out for their career. Stepping up to leadership, therefore, means not only learning to do different things and to think differently about what needs to be done but also learning in different, more self-guided, peer-driven, and external ways. In brief, it means actively

FIGURE 1-5

Expand your network out and across: help for becoming a more effective leader

Looking outside: the percentage of respondents rating each of the following helpful to extremely helpful in becoming a more effective leader

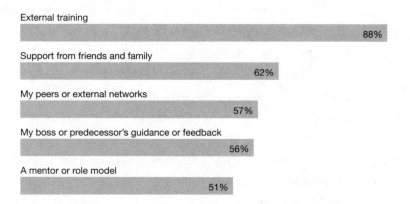

External training — 88%

Support from friends and family — 62%

My peers or external networks — 57%

My boss or predecessor's guidance or feedback — 56%

A mentor or role model — 51%

Source: Author's survey of 173 INSEAD executive program alumni, conducted in October 2013.

creating a network from which you can learn as much as, if not more than, you can from your boss.

Chapter 3 shows how much good leadership depends on having the right network of professional relationships. It discusses how to branch out beyond the strong and comforting ties of friends and colleagues to connect to people who can help you see your work and yourself in a different light. Even if you don't yet value networking activities, are swamped with more immediate job demands, and suspect anyhow that networking is mostly self-serving manipulation, a few simple steps will demonstrate why you can't afford not to build connective advantage.

Be More Playful with Your Self

To really change what he does and the network he relies on to do it, Jacob would have to play around a bit with his own ideas about himself. Both the scope of his job and the nature of his working relationships were a product of his self-concept—his likes and dis-likes, strengths and weaknesses, stylistic preferences and comfort zone. Now he needed to shift from his familiar, hands-on, and di-rective leadership style to a style in which he would delegate more of the day-to-day work to his team and begin to collaborate more extensively with the other divisions. The improved empowerment and communication he had been trying so hard to implement didn't stick, because they clashed with his sense of authentic self.

To an even greater extent than doing a different job and estab-lishing a different network of work relationships, people in transi-tion to bigger leadership roles must reinvent their own identities. They must transform how they see themselves, how others see them, and what work values and personal goals drive their actions.

While the personal transformation typically involves a shift in leadership style, it is much more than that. Consider the follow-ing: 50 percent of the managers I surveyed responded "somewhat or very true" to the statement "My leadership style sometimes gets in the way of my success." In Jacob's case, he admitted that if results lagged behind his expectations, he would often leap into the situation without allowing the team members the time and space to arrive at their own solution. When managers like Jacob are asked to consider what is holding them back from broadening their stylistic repertory, many almost invariably reveal an un-flinching results orientation and commitment to delivering at all costs. This orientation not only has made them successful but also constitutes the core of their professional identities. The managers want to change, but the change is not who they truly are.

For example, among the competencies rated as most critical for effective leaders, my survey respondents listed "motivating and inspiring" as the second-most important. Jacob also listed the same, although he was not rated very highly by his team on this capacity. Motivation and inspiration, however, aren't tools you can select out of a toolbox by, say, increasing your communication to keep people better informed. Instead, the capacity to motivate and inspire depends much more on your ability to infuse the work with meaning and purpose for everyone involved.[16] When this capability doesn't come naturally, you tend to see it as an exercise in manipulation. Likewise, coming to grips with the political realities of organizational life and managing them effectively and authentically are among the biggest hurdles of transitioning to a bigger leadership role.[17] Although many of the aspiring leaders whom I teach cite the ability to influence without authority as a critical competence, many leaders are not as effective as they might be at it, because they view the exercise of influence as playing politics.

Things like stretching outside your stylistic comfort zone and reconciling yourself to the inherently political nature of organizational life, in turn, require a more playful approach than what you might adopt if you see it as "working on yourself." When you're playing with various self-concepts, you favor exploration, withholding commitment until you know more about where you are going. You focus less on achievement than on learning. If it doesn't work for you, then you try something else instead.

Chapter 4 explains why trying to adapt to many of the challenges involved in greater leadership roles can make you feel like an impostor. No one wants to lose herself in the process of change, yet the only way to start thinking like a leader is to act like one, even when it feels inauthentic at first. This chapter shows how you can stop straitjacketing your identity in the guise of authenticity. The outsight you gain from trying to be someone you're not (yet) helps you more than any introspection about the leader you might become.

Stepping Up

Stepping up to play a bigger leadership role is not an event or an outcome. It's a process that you need to understand to make it pay off.

Self-Assessment: Is Your Work Environment Telling You It's Time to Change?

		YES	NO
1.	My industry has changed a lot over the past few years.	_____	_____
2.	My company's top leadership has changed.	_____	_____
3.	My company has grown or reduced significantly in size recently.	_____	_____
4.	We are undergoing a major change effort.	_____	_____
5.	We have new competitors we did not have a few years ago.	_____	_____
6.	Technology is changing how we do business.	_____	_____
7.	I need to interact with more stakeholders to do my job.	_____	_____

Between realizing that you're in a do-it-yourself transition and actually experiencing the accumulated benefits of the new outsights you're getting lies a stepping-up process that is less linear than what you would expect. The transition involved is rarely the upward and onward progression you'd like; nor does it tend to unfold according to any theoretical logic. The transition moves forward and then falls backward repeatedly, but at some point, if you learn enough along the way, the transition sustains its momentum.

	YES	NO
8. I have been in the same job for more than two years.	_____	_____
9. I have been sent for leadership training.	_____	_____
10. Our business is becoming much more international.	_____	_____

Total Score

Assess whether your work environment is telling you it's time to change by totaling the number of "yes" responses:

8–10 Your environment is changing dramatically, and your leadership must change accordingly.

4–7 Your environment is changing in important ways, and with it, the expectations for you to step up to leadership are growing.

3 or below Your environment is experiencing moderate shifts; prepare for changing expectations of you.

Most of the leadership books written for people who want to get from A to B simply tell you what B is: what great leadership looks like. Or, they tell you how to identify a good B for you and then how to measure the gap between your current A and that B. Then they give you a few simple tactics that supposedly will help you fill the gap. Few of the books guide you through the complications in between.

The complex step-up process is the subject of chapter 5. Describing the predictable sequence of stages that change the way you think about A and B, the chapter prepares you for the complications that will inevitably arise in between. It helps you get unstuck when problems arise (they will) and builds a foundation that sustains more enduring changes. You've succeeded in stepping up when the bigger changes that ensue are driven by a new clarity of self that is informed by your direct leadership experience.

How much are you like Jacob? How much has the way you work evolved over the past couple of years? How about your network—is it growing and extending beyond the usual suspects? And how much are you willing to challenge the way you see yourself? The action and thinking shifts that all of us, like Jacob, must make as we step up to bigger leadership roles are the subject of the next four chapters.

Jack Welch famously said, "When the rate of change outside exceeds the rate of change inside, the end is in sight."[18] Before you read ahead, take a moment to evaluate the extent to which changes in your work environment signal that the time has come for a do-it-yourself transition (see the sidebar "Self-Assessment: Is Your Work Environment Telling You It's Time to Change?").

CHAPTER I SUMMARY

✓ To step up to leadership, you have to learn to think like a leader.

✓ The way you think is a product of your past experience.

✓ The only way to change how you think, therefore, is to do different things.

✓ Doing things—rather than simply thinking about them—
will increase your outsight on what leadership is all about.

✓ Outsight comes from a "tripod" of sources: new ways
of doing your work (your job), new relationships (your
network), and new ways of connecting to and engaging
people (yourself).

✓ Sustainable change in your leadership capacity requires
shifts on all three legs of the tripod.

Redefine Your Job

WHEN I ASK THE MANAGERS and other professionals who attend my classes how many of them are involved in creating change of some sort in their organizations, close to 90 percent raise their hands. When I ask the same managers about the results of their efforts, most admit that the results leave much to be desired. Inertia, resistance, habitual routines, and entrenched cultures slow the participants' progress at every turn.

There is no doubt that the capacity to lead change is at the top of the list of leadership competencies. But in today's fast-paced and resource-constrained environment, many of us are delivering 100 percent on the current demands of our jobs. Not only is there little time to think about the current business, but we cannot easily carve out the time to sense new trends coming down the line or to develop ourselves further for a future move. That's why a majority of the mangers I surveyed said that routine and operational aspects of their work consume too much of their time.

One of my executive MBA students recently told me, "I know that I have to carve out more time to think strategically about my company's business, but all my peers are executing to the hilt and I don't want to fall behind." Prompted to describe her predicament, she was at a loss to explain what she should be doing

FIGURE 2-1

Increasing your outsight by redefining your job

OUTSIGHT COMES FROM ACTION

REDEFINE
YOUR JOB
YOUR NETWORK
YOUR SELF

OUTSIGHT

instead. She just knew that she was limiting her contribution by merely responding to the many client requests getting pushed down to her level without stopping to consider how the pieces fell together or how to prioritize directives coming down the line. But she didn't dare stop, because everyone around her was continuing to push on the operational front.

What does it mean to take a more strategic approach to our jobs? Boiled down to its essence, strategy entails knowing what to do among the many things competing for our attention, how to get it done, and why. Unfortunately, the way most of us do our work leaves little room for this kind of strategic thinking.

Consider your typical work routine. For most of the managers I meet, the day usually begins with a quick check of the most urgent emails, followed by a round of long, routine, and often boring meetings and conference calls with the team or key customers. Incessant travel and dealing with the chronic talent shortages and high turnover of the emerging markets or the retrenchment of the more mature ones adds an unprecedented burden of overwork. With a multiplication of corporate initiatives, compliance procedures, and urgent requests from all corners, the responsibilities pile on. At the end of a long day, the inbox is full again and the requested reports (or budgets or analyses) have yet to be finished. There is little time to think about why you do what you do, about the meaning and purpose of your work beyond the immediate deliverables. It's no wonder routine crowds out strategy.

This chapter is about how to apply the outsight principle to adopt a more strategic approach to your work, whether you are taking charge in a new role or simply stepping up to leadership within the confines of your current position. It will show you how to reallocate your time to prioritize unfamiliar and nonroutine activities that will increase your capacity to act more strategically through a wider view of your business, your group's place in the larger organization, and your work's contribution to outcomes that matter (figure 2-1).

Doing the Wrong Things Well

Sophie, a rising star in her firm's supply-chain operation, was stupefied to learn that a radical reorganization of the procurement function was being discussed without her input. Rewarded to date for steady annual improvements, she had consistently delivered on her key performance indicators but failed to notice the competitive shifts in her firm's markets. These shifts were making her firm's historical approach to purchasing and warehousing expensive and ineffective. Nor was she aware of the resulting internal shuffle for resources and power at the higher levels of her company and the extent to which her higher-ups were now pressured to increase cost efficiencies. She was the last to hear about any new imperatives, let alone anticipate them.

Although she had built a loyal, high-performing team, Sophie had few relationships outside her group and even fewer at her boss's level. Putting in long hours to continuously improve her operation left her little time to keep up with the latest trends in supply-chain management. Her function area, the supply chain, was also in the midst of a radical transformation as manufacturers expanded internationally, pursued strategic sourcing, and built more collaborative and sustainable relationships with suppliers. Lacking outsight on innovations in her field, she was blindsided by a proposal from her counterpart in manufacturing.

Her first reaction was defensive. The supply chain was her purview, and her results were impeccable; if a strategic review was in order, she should be the one in charge, she argued. But without the benefit of the broader, cross-functional, and external perspective that her boss expected of someone three years into the job, her ideas were discounted as parochial. Lacking greater strategic insight, she could not form a sellable plan for the future— one that took into account new industry realities and the shifting priorities of her firm.

At first, Sophie thought hard about quitting and moving to a "less political" firm. After all, she was only trying to do the right thing. It seemed to her that the only way to be heard was to spend time schmoozing with senior management instead of getting the job done. Only after some patient coaching from a senior manager did she start to venture outside her cocoon and talk to a broader set of people inside and outside the company. Reluctantly, she conducted a study to learn what other companies were doing. Next, she brought in a consultant to help her narrow down her options. This project brought her in contact with a range of people at her boss's level, across the different divisions of the company. She learned about how they saw the business evolving. Eventually, after a 180-degree turn in how she defined and went about her job, she came to see that a very different supply-chain strategy was indeed required, one that made irrelevant most of what she had built.

Sophie learned the hard way that she was very efficient—at the wrong thing. She was not much different from many successful managers who continue to devote the bulk of their time to doing what they have learned too well. They define their jobs narrowly, in terms of their own areas of expertise, and confine their activities to where they have historically contributed the most value and consistent results. At first, this narrow role is what's expected of them. But over time, expectations shift. To avoid the kind of competency trap Sophie fell into, you need to understand how once-useful mind-sets and operating habits can persist long after they have outlived their usefulness.

Avoid the Competency Trap

We all like to do what we already do well. Sports coaches tell us that amateur golfers spend too much of their time practicing their best swings, at the expense of the aspects of their game that need more work. Likewise, every year, we see the downfall of yet another company that was once the undisputed leader in a given product, service, or technology, but that missed the boat when a new, disruptive technology came along.[1]

That is precisely what happens when we let the operational "day job" crowd out our engagement in more strategic, higher-value-added activities. Like athletes and companies, managers and professionals overinvest in their strengths under the false assumption that what produced their past successes will necessarily lead to future wins.

Eventually we become trapped in well-honed routines that no longer correspond to the requirements of a new environment.

Consider Jeff, a general manager for a beverage company subsidiary. A star salesman before he became a star sales manager, Jeff also succeeded as country head in two successive assignments, both positions in which the general manager's job was actually a mega–sales manager position, and the business required a turnaround. His third assignment, in Indonesia, looked like more of the same, albeit at a larger scale and scope. After two years of implementing what everyone regarded as a successful turnaround strategy, Jeff was sure that his results had put him squarely in the running for senior management. But no new assignment was in sight, and a poor performance review hinted that Jeff's bosses were starting to expect something else from him.

What was going on? Although Jeff was still delivering results as before, his bosses now wanted to know more about his capacity to lead at a higher level. All the indicators left them doubtful.

For starters, it was becoming obvious that he was on the verge of losing his head of sales and marketing. Rajiv was the only person in the operation with the technological expertise required to develop and implement the company's new digital strategy in its local market. The extroverted and relationship-oriented Jeff had little patience with the IT and data issues that consumed his highly analytical Indian marketing chief, and the cultural differences between the two men only made their communication harder. Rajiv saw his job as aligning new marketing technologies with business goals, serving as a liaison to the centralized brand groups, evaluating and choosing technology providers, and helping craft new digital business models. Jeff wanted Rajiv to devote more time to managing relationships with the group's distributors, the cornerstone of his strategy, and felt that Rajiv was neglecting his sales responsibilities. Every time they spoke, the conversation ended in a stalemate. Unbeknownst to him, Jeff's managers worried that he was ill equipped to manage the diverse teams he would encounter in a higher-level assignment.

Jeff's bosses were also displeased by the way he routinely ignored corporate initiatives and failed to keep the brand and staff functions informed and involved. Earlier, Jeff's superiors had shown more patience with his lone-ranger tactics, because the turnarounds he had been asked to pull off called for speedy and decisive action. Now his bosses were curious to see if he could adapt to changing circumstances. The Indonesian operation was in the black again, thanks to Jeff's tried-and-true approach. E-commerce initiatives were forcing leaders to grapple with some of the responsibilities that typically fell to marketing, such as how to deliver brand messages directly via the web. But Jeff continued to define the local strategy pretty much in terms of sales, neglecting the views and priorities of his peers in the company's corporate staff.

Not surprisingly, the leadership bench in Indonesia remained underdeveloped. Jeff routinely stifled his team's development by intervening in the details of their work, "adding too much value," as leadership coach Marshall Goldsmith jokingly describes this sort of micromanagement.[2] Jeff was starting to itch for a new challenge, but unfortunately, he had made himself so indispensable that there was no one ready to succeed him. Let's analyze how Jeff had gotten himself into a competency trap.

We enjoy what we do well, so we do more of it and get still better at it. The more we do something, the more expert we become at it and the more we enjoy doing it. Such a feedback loop motivates us to get even more experience. The mastery we feel is like a drug, deepening both our enjoyment and our sense of self-efficacy.[3] It also biases us to believe that the things we do well are the most valuable and important, justifying the time we devote to them. As one unusually frank, high-potential manager told me, it can be hard to do otherwise: "I annoy a lot of people by not being sympathetic to their priorities. It's feedback I've had throughout my career: you work on things you like and think are important. It is a problem. It can seem disrespectful. Do I want to work on it? I should but probably never will."

It was much the same for Jeff, who found himself solving other people's problems over and over again. When his managers failed to build relationships with key clients, Jeff stepped in. When accounts were not settled, he rushed to the rescue. Instead of working through his team, he was working for them. "I can't sit still if I see a problem that could have real financial consequences," Jeff would say. "I need to hammer away at it until things get done correctly."

His direct reports teased him for this: they made him a "Jeff's hierarchy of needs" diagram, based on Abraham Maslow's famous pyramid (figure 2-2).[4] Below the bottom rung (physiological needs),

FIGURE 2-2

Jeff's "hierarchy of needs" pyramid

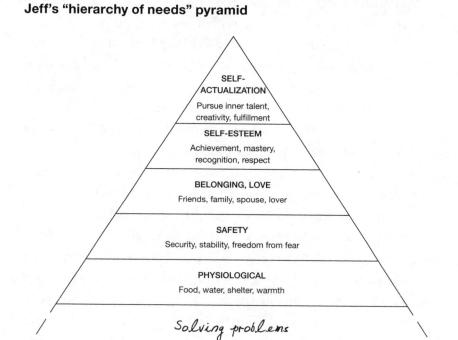

32

they had drawn another, titled "Solving problems." Jeff liked the diagram; it reflected how he liked to see himself. When he was solving problems, his most basic needs were met: he felt valuable, decisive, competent, and in control of the ultimate outcome.

When we allocate more time to what we do best, we devote less time to learning other things that are also important. The problem isn't just what we are doing; it's what we're neglecting to do (and not learning to do) instead. Because experience and competence work together in a virtuous (or vicious) cycle, when that competence is in demand, as it often is, it invites further utilization. So some leadership muscles get very strong while others remain underdeveloped.

Jeff, like many successful managers, was focusing too much on the details—particularly in his domain of functional expertise—and micromanaging his teams so that he single-handedly drove performance. What was he failing to do? A lot. He wasn't strategizing for the more stable medium term made possible by his successful turnaround. He wasn't taking into account the views and priorities of his corporate support functions. He wasn't having difficult conversations with key members of his team or coaching them through the issues that got them in over their heads. He wasn't keeping his far-off boss adequately informed. It's not that Jeff was unable to do any of these things; he just didn't know how to do them in a way that didn't seem like a huge time sink.

Over time, it gets more costly to invest in learning to do new things. The better we are at something, the higher the opportunity cost of spending time doing something else. The returns from exploiting what we already do well are more certain and closer in time and space than the returns from exploring potential new areas in which we will necessarily feel weak at first.[5] This self-reinforcing property of learning makes people sustain their current focus in the short term.

How Do You Spend Your Time?

A team of Harvard Business School researchers set out to discover how bosses spend their time.[a] They asked the administrative assistants of the chief executives of ninety-four Italian firms to record their activities for a week. What did the executives spend the most time on? You guessed it: they spent 60 percent of their time in meetings.

Years earlier, a classic study compared managers who were rated highly effective by their own teams with managers who were successful in moving up to higher positions.[b] The biggest difference between the two groups of managers was how they spent their time. The effective managers spent most of their time working with their direct reports inside their teams. The successful managers spent much more time on networking activities with peers in other units and higher-ups throughout the organization.

Even if you don't have the luxury of an assistant, in this age of apps, it's easy to track what you spend your time on, at work and at home. Start by simply observing what you do in a typical week. You might, for example, track how much time you spend alone in your office and inside versus outside your department. You can use tools like these to keep tabs on your time:[c]

Perversely, the trap is sprung precisely because we are delivering on our results. When we are reaching and exceeding the goals our bosses have set for us, many will conspire to keep us where we are because we can be relied upon to perform. And they will justify their self-serving decision by pointing out that we have not shown enough leadership potential.

Jeff was so busy solving problems as they arose that he never stopped to put in place clear operating guidelines and performance

Toggl and ATracker: These apps let you track anything you do; you simply tap on your phone to start or stop each activity. ATracker's reports show how much time you are spending on routine tasks and formal activities like meetings.

TIME Planner: This app combines scheduling and time tracking features. You can schedule some reflection time at 1 p.m., for example, then be reminded to do it, and then register whether you've actually done it.

My Minutes: This app helps you meet your time management goals. If you resolve to spend at most forty-five minutes on a presentation, for example, the app tells you when you're out of time and when you've hit your goal.

a. Oriana Bandiera, Luigi Guiso, Andrea Prat, and Raffaella Sadun, "What Do CEOs Do?" working paper 11-081 (Boston: Harvard Business School, 2011).

b. Fred Luthans, "Successful vs. Effective Real Managers," *Academy of Management Executive* 2, no. 2 (1988): 127–132.

c. Adapted from Laura Vanderkam, "10 Time-Tracking Apps That Will Make You More Productive in 2014," *Fast Company*, January 6, 2014, www .fastcompany.com/3024249/10-time-tracking-apps-that-will-make-you-more-productive-in-2014.

objectives to guide his team. He failed to notice that his successful market strategy had run its course and that the operation needed a new post-turnaround direction. His constant intervention undermined the development of his key talents two or three layers below. Instead of working through his team, he was working for them. All this came at a cost: although he was working 24-7, neither his team nor his superiors were happy.

Because most of us come to define our jobs in terms of our core strengths and skills, similar versions of this story play out whenever we are asked to move from the familiar to the unfamiliar. We have difficulty making the transition from work firmly rooted in our own functional knowledge or expertise to work that depends on guiding diverse parties, many outside our direct control, to a shared goal—that is, the work of leadership. The sidebar "How Do You Spend Your Time?" illustrates the importance of making this transition.

Understand What Leaders Really Do

What muscles should Jeff be strengthening instead? To answer this question, first consider the age-old distinction between *management* and *leadership*.[6] At its essence, management entails doing today's work as efficiently and competently as possible within established goals, procedures, and organizational structures. Leadership, in contrast, is aimed at creating change in what we do and how we do it, which is why leadership requires working outside established goals, procedures, and structures and explaining to others why it's important to change—even when the reasons may be blatantly obvious to us.

When doing our routine work, we're asking, "How can we do the work better (i.e., faster, in a less costly way, with higher quality)?" We spend our time with our teams and current customers, or on our individual contributions, executing on plans and goals to which we have committed. We usually know what we'll get for the time, effort, and resources we invest. We have faith that we'll meet our goals because we are using the skills and procedures that have worked for us in the past.

When doing leadership work, we're asking, "What should we be doing instead?" We spend our time on things that might not have any immediate payoff and may not even pay off at all. For example, we might be looking beyond our normal functions to envision a different future. Because transformation is always more uncertain than incremental progress (or decline), belief in the rightness of a new direction requires a leap of faith. We are more inclined to take the leap when the change engages us and when we buy into not only what the leaders do but, more importantly, who they are and what they stand for. In other words, to act like leaders, we will have to devote much of our time to the following practices:

- Bridging across diverse people and groups

- Envisioning new possibilities

- Engaging people in the change process

- Embodying the change

Become a Bridge

Consider the conventional wisdom about how to lead a team effectively: set clear goals; assign clear tasks to members; manage the team's internal dynamics and norms; communicate regularly; pay attention to how members feel, and give them recognition; and so on. These are important things to do, but they may not make much of a difference to your results.

In study after study over more than twenty years, MIT professor Deborah Ancona and her colleagues have consistently debunked this widespread belief about effective team leadership.[7] They found that the team leaders who delivered the best results did not spend the bulk of their time playing these internal roles. Instead, the best leaders worked as bridges between the team and its external environment. They spent much of their time outside, not inside the team. They went out on reconnaissance, made sure the right information and resources were getting to the team, broadcasted accomplishments selectively, and secured buy-in from higher up when things got controversial. Moreover, successful leaders monitored what other teams—potential competitors, potential teams from whom they could learn and not reinvent the wheel—were doing.

Take, for example, a former BP manager named Vivienne Cox. When she took charge of a newly formed Gas, Power & Renewables group, she inherited a number of small, "futuristic" but peripheral businesses, including solar and wind energy and hydrogen gas. A neophyte on alternative energy, Cox gathered inputs from a broad group of outsiders to her group and company to analyze the business environment and to brainstorm ideas. These conversations brought to light the urgency of moving away from a purely petroleum-based business model.[8]

Cox is a classic example of the leader as a bridge between her team and the relevant parties outside the team. She chose a "number two," who was complementary to her in his focus on internal and company processes, while she herself maintained a strategic, external, and inspirational role. She spent much of her time of talking to key people across and outside the firm to develop a strategic perspective on the nature of the threats and opportunities facing her nascent group and to sell the emerging notion of low-carbon power to then CEO John Browne and her peers. Her network included thought leaders in a range of sectors (more on this in chapter 3). She placed outsiders like her strategic adviser in key roles to transcend a parochial view. And Cox brought in key BP peers like the heads of technology and China to make sure her team was also informed by those who saw the world with a different lens.

Once she had a strategic direction in mind for her alternative-energy business, Cox activated her network to spread "sound bites" about the alternative energy industry across the company. She explained: "It can be so helpful to make a comment here, have a conversation there—it's the socialisation of facts and ideas, creating a buzz. It's much more important than presentations. If it works well, you create a demand for the information—they come to you to ask for more."[9]

Another good example is Jack Klues, former CEO of Vivaki, the media-buying arm of Publicis Groupe. Publicis had consolidated many separate media operations to increase its purchasing power with the likes of Google and Yahoo and to consolidate expertise in digital advertising. The job entailed weaving together disparate talents to exploit the new economies of scale. Klues described his role: "I've always thought my job was to be a 'connector.' I see myself as connecting interesting and smart pieces in new and different ways . . . I was the one person about whom the other twenty media directors could say: 'Yeah, we'll work for him.' And I think they all thought they were smarter than me in their particular areas, and they were probably right. But the job was about bringing the parts together. I didn't get the job, because I knew something they didn't know, and that something became the Holy Grail."[10]

Table 2-1 outlines two contrasting roles team leaders play. When you play a hub role, your team and customers are at the center of your work; when you play a bridge role, as Cox did, you work to link your team to the rest of the relevant world. Both roles

TABLE 2-1

Are you a hub or a bridge?

Hub roles	Bridge roles
• Set goals for the team • Assign roles to your people • Assign tasks • Monitor progress toward goals • Manage team member performance; conduct performance evaluations • Hold meetings to coordinate work • Create a good climate inside the team	• Align team goals with organizational priorities • Funnel critical information and resources into the team to ensure progress toward goals • Get the support of key allies outside the team • Enhance the external visibility and reputation of the team • Get recognition for good performers and place them in great next assignments

are critical. What role was Jeff playing? He was clearly a hub. But when people rate the effectiveness of leaders, guess which ones come out on top? The bridges. Leaders who focus on the right-hand column outperform the leaders on the left at nearly every turn.

No matter what kind of organization you work in, team leaders who scout ideas from outside the group, seek feedback from and coordinate with a range of outsiders, monitor the shifting winds within the organization, and obtain support and resources from top managers are able to build more innovative products and services faster than those who dedicate themselves solely to managing inside the team. Part of the secret of their success is that all their bridging activity gives them the outsight they need to develop a point of view on their business, see the big picture organizationally, and set direction accordingly.

Do the "Vision Thing"

Of course, a leader can form a bridge across boundaries but still focus on the wrong things. Even so, the external perspective gained by redefining your work more broadly is a key determinant of whether you, as the leader, will have good strategic ideas. More importantly, an external perspective helps you translate your ideas into an attractive vision of the future for your team and organization.

Broad vision is not an obvious job requirement for many people, including former US president George H. W. Bush. When asked to look away from the short-term, specific goals of his campaign and start focusing on a future to which his voters might aspire, he famously replied, "Oh—you mean the vision thing?"

Although Bush derided the idea of broad vision and although execution-focused managers underplay its importance, the ability to envision possibilities for the future and to share that vision with others distinguishes leaders from nonleaders. Large-scale

What Does It Mean to Have Vision?

Across studies and research traditions, vision has been found to be a defining feature of leadership. But what does it look like in action? The following capabilities or practices are some specific ways good leaders develop vision.[a]

Sensing Opportunities and Threats in the Environment

- Simplifying complex situations

- Seeing patterns in seemingly unconnected phenomena

- Foreseeing events that may affect the organization's bottom line

Setting Strategic Direction

- Encouraging new business

- Defining new strategies

- Making decisions with an eye toward the big picture

Inspiring Others to Look beyond Current Practice

- Asking questions that challenge the status quo

- Being open to new ways of doing things

- Bringing an external perspective

a. Manfred F. R. Kets de Vries, Pierre Vrignaud, Elizabeth Florent-Treacy, and Konstantin Korotov, "360-degree feedback instrument: An overview," *INSEAD Working Paper*, 2007.

surveys by the likes of leadership gurus James Kouzes and Barry Posner bear out this observation.[11] Most people can easily describe what is inadequate, unsatisfactory, or meaningless about what they are doing. But they stay stuck in their jobs for lack of vision of a better way.

Just what does it mean to be visionary? Most everyone agrees that envisioning involves creating a compelling image of the future: what could be and, more importantly, what you, as a leader, would like the future to be.[12] But the kind of vision that takes an organization forward doesn't come from a solitary process of inspired thought. Nor is it about Moses coming down from the mountain with the tablets. It's certainly not the mind-numbing vision statement crafted by the typical organization. The sidebar "What Does It Mean to Have Vision?" lists numerous important capabilities that contribute to true strategic vision.

Let's examine how Vivienne Cox acquired her vision. Her prior role had been to run BP's oil and gas trading operation according to clear-cut, BP-specified performance indicators and planning processes. In her new role, she had to decide what to do about all the bits and pieces of alternative-energy business that had sprouted around the edges of the organization and see if they might fit together. After much bridging to external sources of insight—and this included asking herself and key stakeholders whether BP should, as a big oil company, be in the alternative-energy business—she and her team started to coalesce around a low-carbon future that made sense at BP. Cox next asked, "What should be our ambition?" The conversations that ensued focused on where to compete and on what basis the Alternative Energy group might expect to win. Only much later did her group develop business plans specifying targets such as deal volume and market share.

As Cox's example shows, crafting a vision entails developing and articulating an aspiration. Strategy involves using that aspiration to guide a set of choices about how to best invest time and resources to produce the result you actually want. Both are a far cry from participating in the organization's annual planning process, as Roger Martin, former dean of the University of Toronto's Rotman School of Management, has repeatedly explained.[13] In annual planning, there is a clear process for producing and presenting a document consisting of a list of initiatives with their associated time frames and assigned resources. At best, an annual plan produces incremental gains. Envisioning the future is a much more dynamic, creative, and collaborative process of imagining a transformation in what an organization does and how it does it.

Many successful and competent managers are what I call vision-impaired. In the 360-degree assessments of the managers who come to my programs, envisioning the future direction of the company is one of the dimension of leadership competency on which most participants invariably fall short, compared with other skills such as team building and providing rewards and feedback.[14] Figure 2-3, taken from a summary of feedback from 427 executives and 3,626 observers, shows the notable gap between how these managers see themselves and how the people they work with—juniors, peers, and seniors—view the managers with respect to vision. The gap between the managers' self-perceptions of their envisioning skills and the views of their superiors is even bigger.

Asked to explain the gap, many managers say that their job is to implement what comes down from the top. They believe that strategy and vision are the purview of senior managers and outside consultants who formulate grand plans and then hand them off for execution to the rest of the organization.

Historically, strategy and vision were indeed handed down from the top. But technology has profoundly altered that neat division of labor, eliminating many of the tasks—performance monitoring, instant feedback, and reports and presentations—that were staples of managerial work even five years ago. Increasingly, executives are required to shift their emphasis from improving current operations

FIGURE 2-3

Mind the gap: 360-degree assessment of leadership competencies

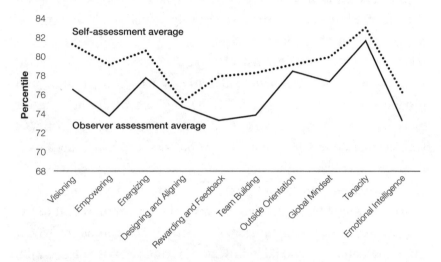

Note: Table based on a sample of 427 executive education participants and their 3,626 observers. "Envisioning the Future," one of the two competencies (along with "Empowering") with the lowest scores and largest gap between the self-assessment and observer scores, as compared with other competencies such as "Designing and Aligning" and "Outside Orientation."

and performance indicators to shaping a common understanding of the organization's present environment and its desired future direction. When an empowered front line is in constant contact with customers and suppliers, and these same customers and suppliers increasingly participate in the innovation process, vision and strategy are no longer the exclusive purview of the CEO. Fast-cycle response and coordination depends on the layers of strategists beneath the C-suite. But we'll never figure out vision and strategy if we remain shut up in our offices, as Jacob tried to do.

Engage, Then Lead

No matter how much strategic foresight you might have and how compelling your ideas, if no one else buys in, not much happens. Nor do people buy in for abstract, theoretical reasons;

they buy in because you have somehow connected with them personally.[15]

Kent, a division manager for a tech company that was having trouble adapting to new marketplace realities, learned this lesson the hard way. He had developed a clear and strong point of view about what his company needed to do to provide more integrated solutions for its customers and to better serve some underexploited markets. And he was determined to push his vision through the organization, damn the torpedoes. But he failed to bring people along. One day, he invited a consultant he knew well to sit in the audience as he gave his PowerPoint pitch to a cross-functional team. Kent drove through a long and complicated set of slides and was visibly surprised when his audience alternated between indifference and pushing back on his ideas.

"You heard me say some important things," Kent told the consultant, "but everyone went to sleep. What happened?"

Admitting that the points Kent made were important, the consultant nevertheless told him why people tuned out: "You didn't build any bridges to those who didn't immediately agree with you."

Years later, Kent understood what had gone wrong. "I had a vision," he recalled, "and I was waiting for everyone else to agree. I was not going to put my vision out for revision—it would fly as it was, or not."

Kent hadn't realized that the quality of a leader's idea is not the only thing people consider when making up their minds about whether to engage with the leader. Naive leaders act as if the idea itself is the ultimate selling point. Experienced leaders, on the other hand, understand that the process is just as important, if not more so. How they develop and implement their ideas, and how leaders interact with others in this process, determine whether people become engaged in the leaders' efforts.

A simple formula summarizes what I have concluded are the three key components for success in leading change:

The idea + the process + you = success in leading change

I came to this formula after noticing an interesting pattern in my classes when we analyze a written case study and the effectiveness of the leader-protagonist. My students rarely discuss what the protagonist is actually advocating, and they talk even less about the outcomes his idea has produced.

Process is hugely important not because results are unimportant but because most change efforts have long-term horizons and because results take time. People make up their mind about whether they want to buy in much earlier, while the initiative is still in progress and the jury is still out on its ultimate success. Consciously or unconsciously, they are looking for clues about whether the initiative will succeed and what success means for them, and they use those clues to place their bets.

So, the bulk of people's attention is devoted to the process the leader uses to come up with and implement the idea: Was the leader inclusive or exclusive, participative or directive? Did he or she involve the right people and enough of them? What levers is the leader using, and are they the right ones? Table 2-2 shows how all the classic steps involved in leading change involve personal choices that are based on the leader's stylistic preferences.

All of these "how" facets of the leader's behavior increase (or erode) people's willingness to give the leader the benefit of the doubt and increase (or erode) their faith that eventually the results will follow. In other words, people create a self-fulfilling prophecy: if they have faith in the leader, then they will cooperate and commit, thereby increasing the likelihood of success. Inexperienced leaders don't just overly focus on the idea; they often try to jump directly from the idea to a new structure to support

TABLE 2-2

Steps and styles in leading change

Key steps in leading change[a]	Stylistic choices that influence the change process
• Create urgency	• Where do I get my information?
• Form a guiding coalition	• How much do I involve others?
• Craft a vision	• What people do I involve?
• Communicate the vision	• How many?
• Empower others to act on it	• How will I sell my ideas?
• Secure short-term wins	• What should my role be?
• Embed the change in the organization's systems and processes	• How fast should we go?

a. See John Kotter, "Why Transformation Efforts Fail," *Harvard Business Review* 73, no. 2 (1995): 59–67, for a classic treatment of key steps in leading change.

it without passing through the necessary phase of showing what their initiative looks like and what its desirable results may be. The sidebar "A Tale of Two Chief Diversity Officers" shows the drastically different outcomes that can result when leaders either engage their people or fail to do so.

A Tale of Two Chief Diversity Officers

Probably one of the hardest leadership transitions is the move from a line job with a clear time horizon and financial results to a support role in which the job is to influence those with bottom-line responsibility. It's even harder if the support job involves something that many managers espouse but that is actually at the bottom of their list of priorities, like diversity. That's the situation faced by new diversity officers—the people charged with putting in place a system to help the organization become more diverse and inclusive—and the situation is often made worse if they are novices to the subject. That's also why many companies have implemented diversity initiatives without seeing much by way of results.

Recently I observed two people take charge as diversity chiefs. Both people were in financial services firms, both moving into the role from the business side, and both without experience in this area.

The first, Nia Joynson-Romanzina, the head of global diversity and inclusion at Swiss Re, sought first to find out what the company thought about diversity and how it could think differently.[17] She started by knocking on doors and talking to executive committee members and group board members. "It became very clear that we were divided into two camps," she told me in an interview. "One wanted to get more women in leadership; the other camp said, 'If this is all about women, count me out.' I realized very quickly that this is a very polarizing topic."

But her conversations revealed that a commitment to diversity of thought and opinion was the one thing that brought everyone together. She explained: "That gave me an understanding of the extent to which gender diversity can be polarizing, while the notion of diversity of thought and opinion was something that everybody could buy into. It evolved naturally into a discussion around inclusion."

As she went about her internal discussions, Joynson-Romanzina also identified the key external conferences, working groups, and thought leaders that might inform her approach. She concluded that although Swiss Re was already a diverse company, unconscious biases were discouraging employees from grabbing the next rungs on the ladder or including others in their teams.

A chance to show what was possible came her way when a change-minded, newly appointed CEO of a Swiss Re business decided that although business was going well, the company could benefit from the infusion of new, more diverse talent. He opened up all the most senior management positions, encouraging everyone to apply. Success would mean being more client-centric; a diversity of viewpoints, genders, culture, education, skills, and so on was a key factor in achieving this.

Shortly before applications closed, the CEO noticed the lack of diversity in the list of candidates; virtually no women were applying for the roles. While scratching his head, he consulted with Joynson-Romanzina, who told him to look beyond his existing network. "Women are less likely to feel qualified, even when they are," she explained. "You need to go out and tell women, and men, very specifically that they should be applying. There is no guarantee that they will get the job, but they should at least apply."

He did just that, extending the application deadline to allow the effort to take effect. A diverse hiring team was brought on board and put through training about unconscious bias. Also, Joynson-Romanzina was invited into the room to join the decision making to challenge any unconscious biases and to ensure an equal playing field for all.

The CEO ended up with an executive group with much greater cross-functionality and generational balance and a female representation of over 40 percent, up from 17 percent before the exercise. In each position, the best person won the job, and there was consensus on that.

This very visible win formed the basis of Joynson-Romanzina's vision and strategy to address diversity shortfalls and enhance the inclusion of employees. While many companies begin by setting numerical targets, she concluded that starting with a numbers focus would raise resistance and distract from the fundamental and long-term change that had to happen. "This is about changing mind-sets," she said. "Include first, and the numbers will follow."

The second diversity officer took a very different tack. She wanted to get the vision right first. For her, this meant taking inventory of what was currently in place across the widespread niches of the organization and how that mapped onto what the research was saying. Of course, she found many inconsistent practices and a great lack of coherence in what the firm was doing.

So, her first priority was to create a model to integrate the different pieces into a holistic framework. She assembled a project group to do just that. The result was a five-part model that included the full diversity landscape, from the business case to a set of cornerstone principles, to all the HR processes in which the principles needed to be embedded. Once she had a best-in-class model, she started to present it to different stakeholders. While many of them applauded the thoroughness of her effort, they weren't quite sure what the goal was or what their part should be.

a. Herminia Ibarra and Nana von Bernuth, "Inclusive Leadership: Unlocking Diverse Talent," *INSEAD Knowledge*, January 15, 2014.

Embody the Change

Of course, there is a big difference between reading about what leaders do and actually observing them in person. Our classroom conversation changes dramatically when we watch a video of the leader in action; the discussion becomes more personal, visceral, and emotional. Often, the participants are at a loss for words to explain their reactions objectively. Judgments now hinge on our personal connection to the leader: "Did I like him? Was he approachable or distant? Did he seem genuine, authentic? Was he listening to the audience, engaging them? Would I want to work with him? Does he speak to me?" Of course, the aha moment is when they realize that others react to them as leaders in the same visceral way.

A big part of stepping up to leadership is recognizing that of the three components of my formula (the idea + the process + you), the *you* part always trumps the idea and is the filter through which people evaluate the process. Your subordinates, peers, and bosses will decide whether your process is fair, whether you have the best interests of the organization in mind (as opposed to simply working to further your career), and whether you actually walk the talk.

What goes into that critically important *you?* Most people have been taught to think that it's all about your management style. But style is only one manifestation of who you are, and many styles can be effective within the same sort of situation. What people are gauging instead has to do with your passion, conviction, and coherence—in other words, your *charisma*, the magic, indefinable word often used to describe great leaders.

Years ago, management professor Jay Conger set out to unveil the mysteries of charisma by getting people to name leaders they found charismatic and then observing what these charismatic leaders did.[16] The leaders were a highly diverse lot in appearance, personality, and leadership style. Some of the charismatic leaders were authoritarian types; others much more collaborative. Some were personable; others, like Steve Jobs, were not. As it turns out, Conger and other researchers who have built on his work found that charisma is less a quality of a person than a quality of a person's relationships with others.[17]

People were seen as charismatic, Conger and others found, when they had compelling ideas that were somehow "right for the times." Because charismatic leaders tend to bridge across organizational groups and external constituents, they are excellent at sensing trends, threats, and opportunities in the environment and therefore able to generate sounder, more appealing ideas. But as we saw above, the idea is only one part of the equation and often the least important. The other attributes of charismatic leaders, Conger and others learned, were all about the process and the leaders themselves. These attributes had to do with how and why charismatic leaders engaged followers and what the leaders found inspiring about who they were as people. Specifically, charismatic leaders have three other things in common:

- Strong convictions based on their personal experience

- Good and frequent communication, mostly through personal stories

- A strong coherence between what they believe, what they
  actually do, and who they are

Take Margaret Thatcher, for example. She is still controversial today, and many people certainly disliked her.[18] But she changed the course of British history by espousing a clear and simple message that she believed in passionately and that was entirely coherent with her formative experiences and personal story.

Thatcher's signature was her legendary skill in the art of political debate. No one could marshal the facts and figures like she did. But all her knowledge and analytical mastery wasn't enough to explain how she managed first to stand out from the pack to break into the highest levels of government and then, as prime minister, to lead her nation through a dramatic turnaround.

What distinguished her from all the other gifted politicians around her was how she used her personal experience to crystallize a powerful political message that she personally embodied. How did she inspire people to act? How did she convey what really mattered to her? She told stories about herself. About how she learned to be thrifty and stick to a budget. About how she was taught not to follow the crowd, but rather to stick to her guns. And she, a grocer's daughter, and a woman at that, attracted a large following of people who believed what she believed.

Did you know that she grew up in a home that had no indoor plumbing? Her father believed in austerity and made no concessions for anything not essential. This and many other formative experiences profoundly shaped Thatcher's beliefs as a politician. She used herself as a metaphor for what she felt was missing in the United Kingdom: a sense of self-determination and redemption through hard work and delayed gratification. She made meaning of her life in a way that aligned with what she wanted the British people to understand and buy into, and it was the meaning she infused into her policies, and not the policies themselves, that got them through.

Simon Sinek, whose TED talk on leadership is one of the most viewed, calls this behavior "working the golden circle." As he explains it, most of us attempt to persuade by talking about what needs to be done and how to do it. We think the secret of persuasion lies in presenting great arguments. Through our logic and mastery, we push our ideas. This doesn't work very well, because we follow people who inspire us, not people who are merely competent. Instead, leaders who inspire action always start with the *why*—their deepest beliefs, convictions, and purpose. In that way, they touch people more deeply. Thus, the *why* lies in the center of the golden circle of inspiration.

Make Your Job a Platform

How do you develop the capacities to bridge different groups, envision a future, engage others, and embody the change? How do you start learning to become a more effective change leader, right now where you are? You start by making your job a platform for doing and learning new things.

Among leaders who have managed to step up, this learning process is nothing like the simpler skill-building process you might employ, say, to improve your negotiation or listening skills. It's a more complex process that involves changing your perspective on what is important and worth doing. So, the best place to begin is by increasing your outsight on the world outside your immediate work and unit by broadening the scope of your job and, therefore, your own horizons about what you might be doing instead.

No matter what your current situation is, there are five things you can do to begin to make your job a platform for expanding your leadership:

- Develop your situation sensors

- Get involved in projects outside your area

- Participate in extracurricular activities

- Communicate your personal why

- Create slack in your schedule

Develop Your Sensors

Leaders are constantly trying to understand the bigger context in which they operate. How will new technologies reshape the industry? How will changing cultural expectations shift the role of business in society? How does the globalization of labor markets affect the organization's recruitment and expansion plans? While a good manager executes flawlessly, leaders develop their outsight into bigger questions such as these. This attention to context requires a well-developed set of sensors that orient you to what is potentially important in a vast sea of information.

Let's return to Sophie, whom we met earlier in this chapter. She got into trouble because her nose was so close to the grindstone that she had no idea what was going on in her company or its markets. Nor was she privy to the political fights being played out above her, the discussions about integrating manufacturing and supply, and the factions that formed around different ways of proceeding.

The more senior you become or the more widespread your responsibilities, the more your job requires you to sense the world around you. Consider the point of view expressed by David Kenny, currently the CEO of The Weather Channel:

A leader has to understand the world. You have to be far more external, more cosmopolitan, have a more global view than

*ever before, to define your company's place in that, its purpose
and value . . . I spend my time with media owners talking
about how they think about digital, Facebook, . . . [and] what
can we do to invent new pricing models. I spend time with
tech companies that support new media. With clients, I am
interested in things like: What did the G20 mean to [them]?
How will all that debt change future generations? I also spend
time with governments . . . I cycle back to clients, I report back
on what I have heard, to help them understand that their networks will move in that direction too.[19]*

How does a more junior leader develop sensors? Salim, who had
worked as an assistant to the president of a large division of a multinational consumer-goods company before his current assignment
as the general manager of a small country in an emerging economy,
attributed his success to his capacity to understand the big picture:

*You need to have a very broad understanding of the business.
Otherwise you get completely lost when the supply chain guy
calls you, speaking to you in "supply-chain-ese," or when the
finance person expects you to understand his language. This
demands a certain capacity for synthesis, because there is a
huge volume of stuff that is going to be hitting you from all
over. If you are not able to very quickly distill and understand
the big themes, you are going to be completely overwhelmed
when your boss suddenly calls and pulls a question you weren't
expecting out of the hat.*

When I asked Salim how he approaches his job, he talked about "developing a nose for the trends" that allowed him to take initiative:

*You can't wait and react all the time. So there are times when
I will go to my boss and say, "Do you realize A, B and C?" And*

he says, "How did you know that?" I say, "I was looking at
this report and that report and thinking about that discussion
we had the last time, and this is what I have picked up in my
conversations." It is a certain capacity to manage information.
You have to have your information system well ordered, so that
when [my boss] calls me and says, "I need an input into this
or that," I am able to convert my knowledge into value-adding
stuff.

Of course, Salim had the benefit of a stint as assistant to the
CEO, a perch from which he could observe how all the dots connected.[20] For those of us whose past experience has been limited
to one function or business unit, the next order of priority is to
find a project that broadens our vision and increases our capacity
to connect the dots. Another method, as we'll see in chapter 3, is
to start working on expanding our networks.

Find a Project Outside Your Area

In my survey about what most helped people step up to leadership, one of the top items was "experience in an internal project
outside my usual responsibilities." All companies have projects
that cut across lines of business, hierarchical levels, and functional specialties. For example, a global product launch can provide exposure to senior leadership, and a cross-functional project
can open doors to new opportunities. Your job is to find out what
these projects are, who's involved, and how to sign up.

François, for example, worked in sales for a multinational
pharmaceutical firm. Although he found his job exciting, it was
not so different from his previous job in another company, and
he looked forward to a promotion as business unit director in
sales and marketing management. Because there were no such
positions available in his company, François crafted for himself

three small projects that increased both his leadership skills and his reputation with his bosses. First, he organized a business meeting for peers in France, where he was based, and in Belgium. As a result, he gained the attention of the area vice president. Next, he created and led a competitive intelligence group for the French affiliate, increasing his visibility at the European level. His work on these two projects raised his profile. Finally, the European medical director named him to a cross-functional group tasked with creating a handbook on how to identify and manage key opinion leaders. His country, France, became a pilot site, and François ran the project.

Many people hesitate to take on extra work. After all, we all struggle to claw back time for our personal lives, and project work almost always comes on top of our day jobs. But when it comes to stepping up to leadership, getting experience across business lines is a better choice than further deepening your skill base within a functional or business silo. One of my students had a great piece of advice for her classmates: "We all managed to make time for our executive MBAs while still doing our day jobs. When the program ends, don't let the day job reabsorb the learning time. Keep that time aside, and use it to evolve your work."

The new skills, the big-picture perspective, the extra-group connections, and the ideas about future opportunities that you gain from temporary assignments like these are well worth the investment. One of my students signed up for a project to rethink best leadership practices at his company, part of an effort to increase engagement and reduce turnover of key employees. Working across the lines showed him how to have influence without formal authority and how his former work habits had stymied talent development. The experience helped him discover an interest in consulting, and he moved into an advisory position two years later.

Indeed, in a world in which hierarchical ascension is being replaced by "jungle-gym careers" consisting of lateral moves, people will progress and develop through their involvement in "hot projects."[21] Such projects involve you in different facets of the business and in new problems that need solving and, ideally, expose you to people who see the world differently than you do.

Participate in Extracurricular Activities

When an internal project is simply not available (or even when it is), professional roles outside your organization can be invaluable for learning and practicing new ways of operating, raising your profile, and, maybe more importantly, revising your own limited view of yourself and improving your career prospects. Let's consider an example.

Robert, a senior policy expert, passionately wanted to run one of his company's businesses and to be held accountable for its P&L. But he wasn't sure he was ready, and he fixated on his own lack of cross-functional experience and limited finance expertise. While his boss, Steve, agreed in principle to find Robert a bigger assignment, Steve shared the same doubts. He had mentored Robert for years, and like many well-intentioned bosses, Steve maintained an outdated view of Robert as the "junior guy."

To prove his merit, Robert only worked harder. It was a busy time for his function as the company prepared to launch an important new product. The birth of his second child had already put a big dent in his external activities, and the new push virtually eliminated any discretionary time for things like the industry conferences he had relied on earlier to stay current. But as he became more and more frustrated about his prospects, he finally changed tack. He decided to get active again to learn about and create alternatives to an internal promotion.

At first Robert wasn't sure where to begin, as many of the external activities he had invested in before would only lead him, at best, to a bigger staff job. One thing he hit on was an industry group focused on innovations in a product niche that his company was also exploring. Leveraging what he knew about what his firm was doing, Robert volunteered to organize a panel. One of the people suggested to him for the panel was an entrepreneur named Thomas, who held the patents for a rapidly growing new product line but who lacked the big-company experience in which Robert was so well versed. They struck up a friendship, and over time, the entrepreneur came to rely more and more on Robert as a sounding board for his organizational dilemmas.

As their relationship developed, Robert came to a newfound appreciation of the extent to which his own knowledge and experience extended beyond the confines of his daily functional responsibilities. This new awareness also had a big effect, indirectly, on how Robert did his job. He became more curious about what other groups in his company were doing, started to ask different questions, became more confident about making suggestions, and reallocated the way he was spending his time to make room for the increasing scope of his external interests. The shift was noticeable to everyone around him, and with time, his boss and peers also came to value Robert's perspective.

No amount of introspection about his strengths and preferences could have given Robert the outsight he gained, thanks to his relationships with Thomas. Ultimately, the self-image that Robert saw reflected in the entrepreneur's eyes helped Robert build the confidence he needed to go after a line role more aggressively and more convincingly.

David, who made the transition from his job as a specialist in project finance and leveraged finance to a leadership position as country manager for a European commercial bank, is another good example of how extracurricular activities can help you grow. His management was happy with the status quo for the foreseeable future, and the recessionary environment in Europe limited his possibilities. Fearing a career plateau, he took two steps. First, he volunteered for a large project at the head office in Frankfurt. The project required him to spend one or two days a week away from his daily work (forcing him to delegate some of the more routine aspects of his job to his team) and connected him with a handful of senior managers he hadn't known before. Second, he joined the Young Presidents' Organization (YPO), where he made some connections that helped him think more creatively about possible next moves. Like Robert, David was ignorant about what kind of curriculum vitae he needed to shift in a different direction, as most of the people in his company had followed a more traditional path. That wasn't the case at the YPO, where he also learned how to frame and sell his expertise in a way that expanded rather than limited his options.

If you are feeling stuck or stale, raise your outsight by participating in industry conferences or other professional gatherings that bring together people from different companies and walks of life. Build from your interests, not just your experience. One of my students, for example, routinely looks for opportunities to speak at conferences on topics related to his experience. He recently gave a talk at his company on life in Nigeria, where he had worked for a number of years, showing a movie about daily life in Lagos, followed by a question-and-answer session with potential candidates for expatriation. These activities have been even more worthwhile than he anticipated: "I found that building your personal brand increases your chances of getting proposals to join strategic initiatives and step out of your day-to-day job for a while."

Teach, speak, or blog on topics that you know something about, or about which you want to learn. And if there isn't something out

Sheryl Sandberg's Side Project

Most of us know Sheryl Sandberg as Facebook's ubiquitous chief operating officer. But what really gave her the visibility she enjoys today originated with a TED talk that had nothing to do with her day job.

Sandberg was a keen observer of her environment. Noticing the scarcity of women in Silicon Valley, she identified several issues that she believed were holding women back in business. She started to share her observations, informally and in small gatherings at first. As her ideas resonated, she was encouraged to take them public. When an opportunity to speak at TED came up, she took it.

The TED talk went viral and led to other invitations, first at a Barnard College graduation and then at Harvard Business School. Just those three talks have been viewed over one million times, a level of impact that few corporate CEOs, apart from Steve Jobs, can boast. Her best-selling book, *Lean In*, followed, and the rest is history.

No one else before had created that level of interest in, and discussion about, issues of women in the workplace. What does this have to do with Sandberg's work leading Facebook? The credibility the book gave her not only helped her recruit more women to Facebook but also landed her a position on Facebook's board and expanded the reach of her network.

there that meets your needs, create your own. A sector manager for an internet commerce organization, for example, created her own community of marketing experts from different organizations by starting a monthly breakfast group. These extracurricular activities can help you see more possibilities, increase your visibility with people who can later help you land the next role or project, and, in the process, as Robert found, motivate you to shed some of the time-consuming tasks and responsibilities that no longer merit so much of your attention. The sidebar "Sheryl Sandberg's Side Project" describes another good example of a fruitful extracurricular activity.

Communicate "Why"

The overwhelming success of the TED conferences and videos has produced a cottage industry of books and workshops that teach people how to do a TED-type talk.[22] People are signing up in droves to learn because communication skills are at a premium today, no matter what we do. As we step up to bigger leadership roles, we find ourselves having to present our ideas more often and to more audiences who don't necessarily share the same assumptions or bases of expertise as our own. So, we have to rely on the least common denominator to get our message across. That is usually a good story.

TED talks have a recipe that anyone can follow. It often starts with a story from the speaker's personal experience; the story illustrates and motivates the main point the person wants to make. Once the audience is hooked by the story, the main points—the technical or scientific bits—are easier to follow and retain. The talk usually ends with the moral of the personal story, reminding the audience that the message, no matter how arcane, is personal. It's embodied.

For example, author Elizabeth Gilbert begins her talk about the nature of creative genius by talking about the predicament in which she found herself after the unexpected success of her book, *Eat, Pray, Love*. Everyone told her, and she herself believed, that she had reached the pinnacle of success in her thirties. It would only be downhill from there. How would she motivate herself to do her job as a writer for the decades to come? She set out to answer

Elements of a Good Story

All great stories, from *Antigone* to *Casablanca* to *Star Wars*, derive their power from a beginning-middle-end story structure and these other basic characteristics:[a]

A protagonist: The listener needs someone to care about. The story must be about a person or group whose struggles we can relate to.

A catalyst: In the beginning, a catalyst is what compels the protagonist to take action. Somehow, the world has changed so that something important is at stake. It's up to the protagonist to put things right again.

Trials and tribulations: In the middle of the story, obstacles produce frustration, conflict, and drama and often lead the protagonist to change in an essential way. As in *The Odyssey*, the trials reveal, test, and shape the protagonist's character. Time is spent wandering in the wilderness, far from home.

A turning point and resolution: Near the end of the story, there comes a point of no return, after which the protagonist can no longer see or do things the same way as before. The protagonist either succeeds magnificently (or fails tragically).

a. Adapted from Herminia Ibarra and Kent Lineback, "What's Your Story?" *Harvard Business Review* 83, no. 1 (2005): 64–71.

that question for herself by researching the creative process. She learned that beliefs about creativity have changed over the centuries, from an archaic view of genius as something that visited a person, to today's view of genius as an innate personal trait. The research helped her understand that we can't set out to produce great creative work directly, because we don't always have control over our inspiration. All we can do is our own part, and that's to work daily and methodically so that we're in place when inspiration comes.

According to psychologist Jerome Bruner, a message is twenty times more likely to be remembered accurately and longer when it is conveyed through a well-constructed story than when it is based on facts or figures. I am not sure what I would have remembered from Gilbert's talk had she simply cited the studies and presented a model about conditions under which creative genius is manifest. But I remember well her story about her daily struggle to write after the literary world declared her an international hit. Seldom is a good story so needed as when we want others to believe what we believe so that they will act as we want them to act. From ancient times the world over, good stories like Gilbert's relate the challenges that test, shape, and reveal the leader's character or purpose.[23] The sidebar "Elements of a Good Story" lays out the very basics that help the storyteller engage the audience.

What do you believe, and how did you come to believe it? The answer lies in your personal story: how you grew up, the experiences that shaped you, the challenging moments when you had to rise to the occasion, the personal failures that taught you important lessons.[24] When we want someone to know us, we share stories of our childhood, our families, our school years, our first loves, the development of our political views, and so on. Why do we buy famous leaders' biographies and autobiographies? We want to know more about their life growing up, about their exploits, triumphs, traumas, and foibles—not the five-point plan they put in place to increase margins. At work, though, it doesn't occur to many of us to reveal our personal sides, and that is a lost opportunity.

You probably already know which stories are your best ones. What you need to learn now is how and when to tell them in the service of your leadership. One way to learn is to pay attention to people who are good at telling stories. What do these storytellers do? It helps even more to practice. One great advantage of the different job-expanding methods outlined above is that they also provide ready-made, live audiences for practicing telling your story.

Any context will do in which you're likely to be asked, "What can you tell me about yourself?" or "What do you do?" or "Where are we going?"[25] Start with your clubs and associations: volunteer to speak at every occasion that comes up. Or, if this is too radical a step, join an organization like Toastmasters, or take a storytelling seminar that will have you practicing in front of a safe audience of strangers. As you get better, seize opportunities inside your organization: a farewell party or the annual off-site. One of my managers happened to take a storytelling class, by serendipity, the week he was scheduled to give a big presentation to his organization. He threw out the PowerPoint presentation he'd assembled and told three stories instead. He told me he had never had such positive feedback on his speaking.

Tell and retell your stories. Rework them as you would work on draft after draft of an epic novel until you've got the right version of your favorites, the one that's most compelling and feels most true to you.

Get Some Slack

Many years ago, a still-unknown management scholar named John Kotter took a handheld camera and followed a bunch of general managers around to see what they actually did (as opposed to what everyone assumed they were doing). The biggest thing that surprised him was how inefficient the most successful managers seemed to be.[26]

Much of their work didn't take place in planned meetings or even inside offices or conference rooms. Often, the work didn't even look like work. Instead they walked around, bumping into people serendipitously, wandering into their offices, hashing out deals in the airport lounge with key customers, and so on. These chance "meetings" were usually very short and often seemed random. But each manager made good use of these impromptu encounters to get information, mention or reinforce an important priority, or further develop his (they were all men at the time) relationships with the people whose paths he crossed. This seemingly unsystematic approach, rather than filling out reports or giving formal presentations, was the successful manager's day job.

Kotter also filmed the managers' agendas. As you might expect, the contrast between the diaries of the more effective managers and those of the less effective ones is striking. But it's not what you might expect. The most effective managers had plenty of slack in their schedule: lots of unscheduled time. The less effective managers had diaries overflowing with meetings, travel, conference calls, and formal presentations.

The new ways of thinking and acting involved in stepping up to leadership require a precious and scarce resource—time. If you're like most of the managers and professionals I teach, routine and immediate demands crowd out the time you need for the more unstructured work of leadership. When you are stretched to the hilt, it's hard to ask yourself, "Am I focusing on the right things?" We fail to build in the necessary slack, precisely because time is short and there is so much to do.

In a recent book titled *Scarcity*, economists Sendhil Mullainathan and Eldar Shafir make an interesting parallel between poverty of money and poverty of time.[27] Both, they show, produce "tunneling," a narrow focus on the short term and a seeming incapacity to delay short-term gratification for the sake of future rewards.

To make the point, Mullainathan and Shafir tell a story about an overstretched acute-care hospital that was always fully booked. With the operating rooms at 100 percent capacity, when emergency cases arose—and they always did—the hospital was forced to bump long-scheduled but less urgent surgeries: "As a result, hospital staff sometimes performed surgery at 2 a.m.; physicians often waited several hours to perform two-hour procedures; and staff members regularly worked unplanned overtime." Because the hospital was constantly behind, it was constantly reshuffling the work, an inefficient and stressful way of operating.

As most organizations in trouble are apt to do, the hospital hired an external consultant who came up with a surprising solution: leave one operating room unused, set aside for unanticipated cases. The hospital administrators responded as most of us would: "We are already too busy, and they want to take something away from us. This is crazy."

Much like the overcommitted person who cannot imagine taking on the additional and time-consuming task of stepping back and reorganizing, let alone giving up a precious resource for something that might or might not occur, the hospital's managers were skeptical. But the operating-room gambit worked. Having an empty room allowed the hospital staff to react to unforeseen emergencies much more efficiently, without having to reschedule everything. It reduced overwork, and the quality of operations improved.

So it is for the overextended manager. It's when we are at our busiest that we most need to free up time so that we can use it for the nonroutine and the unexpected. In this way, we increase our capacity to lead, as Kotter's effective general managers did.

Add Before You Subtract

There are two very different kinds of problems in allocating your time to leadership work. The first, a difficult but tractable problem, is making yourself spend more time on the things you know are really important, but not urgent. This is hard to do, but there are tried-and-true techniques for doing so.[28] The second, harder problem is changing your views about what is important.

The only way to tackle this second problem is to get involved in activities that will make you think differently about what you should be doing and why: boundary-spanning roles that make you more attuned to the environment outside your team, projects outside your main area of expertise, and activities outside your firm. These are medium-term investments without immediate payoff, so as you add them, you won't be able to subtract much of what you used to do—just yet. The sidebar "Getting Started: Experiments with Your Job" offers ways for overextended managers to step out of their unproductive routines. Only when the new roles start to pay off will you be motivated and able to start letting go of the old ones.

GETTING STARTED

Experiments with Your Job

> ❯ *In the next three days, start observing someone whom you consider a strategic thinker or visionary leader. Learn how he thinks and communicates.*

> ❯ *Over the next three weeks, find a project (inside or outside your organization) outside your area of expertise, and sign up for it.*

> ❯ *Over the next three months, watch some TED talks. Pay specific attention to how people tell their story to underscore the point they want to make. In your domain, find leaders who are also good at telling stories to make a point, and listen to how they do it. Sign up for a course in storytelling.*

CHAPTER 2 SUMMARY

✓ Success creates competency traps. We fall into a competency trap when these three things occur:

- You enjoy what you do well, so you do more of it and get yet better at it.

- When you allocate more time to what you do best, you devote less time to learning other things that are also important.

- Over time, it gets more costly to invest in learning to do new things.

✓ To act like a leader, you must devote time to four tasks you won't learn to do if you are in a competency trap:

- Bridging across diverse people and groups.

- Envisioning new possibilities.

- Engaging people in the change process.

- Embodying the change.

✓ It's hard to learn these things directly and especially without the benefit of a new assignment. So, no matter what your current situation is, there are five things you can do to begin to make your job a platform for expanding your leadership:

- Develop your situation sensors.

- Get involved in projects outside your area.

- Participate in extracurricular activities.

- Communicate your personal "why."

- Create slack in your schedule.

Network Across and Out

O N A SCALE OF ONE TO FIVE, how important is having a good network to your ability to accomplish your goals? When I ask my executive students this question, most of them answer in the fours and fives. Even the most naive of them agree that, like it or not, relationships hold the key to both their current capacity and future success.

What can a network do for you? It can keep you informed. Teach you new things. Make you more innovative. Give you a sounding board to flesh out your ideas. Help you get things done when you are in a hurry and you need a favor. The list goes on.[1]

When it comes to stepping up to leadership, your network is a tool for identifying new strategic opportunities and attracting the best people to them. It's the channel through which you sell your initiatives to the people you depend on for cooperation and support. It's what you rely on to win over the skeptics. It protects you from being clueless about the political dynamics that so often kill good ideas. Your relationships are also the best way to change with your environment and industry, even if your formal role or assignment has not changed. Without a good network, you will also limit your own imagination about your own career prospects. Your network is also what puts you on the radar screen

FIGURE 3-1

Increasing your outsight by networking across and out

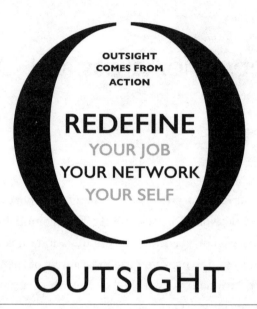

OUTSIGHT COMES FROM ACTION

REDEFINE
YOUR JOB
YOUR NETWORK
YOUR SELF

OUTSIGHT

of people who control your next job or assignment and who form their opinion of your potential partly on who knows you and what they say about you. In short, your network is a crucial source of outsight on your job—and everything else to which you aspire (figure 3-1).

But just because a person knows that a network is important to her success, it doesn't mean she is devoting sufficient time and energy to making it useful and strong. In fact, few of us do. I know because I ask a second question: On a scale of one to five, how would you rate the quality of your current network?

My guess is that your second number is lower than your first. On average, my executive students answer this question in the twos and threes. Most admit that even by their own standards, their networks of connections leave much to be desired.

This chapter is about how to change that. We'll start by looking at how your attitude toward networking limits your potential to build important relationships and how your current network traps you in old mind-sets. Next, we'll examine how the three key properties of networks either propel you forward or hold you back. Then, we'll map out the steps you need to increase your capacity to lead through a broad and diverse network of relationships.

We'll start by assessing the network you have today. The sidebar "A Network Audit" lets you conduct a quick-and-dirty audit of your present network. The questions represent a short version of the survey I use with my students.[2]

We're All Narcissistic and Lazy

Indulge me in answering the following quiz question: Of the following, which do you think is the primary determinant of chemistry in a professional relationship, according to social science research? Pick one among the following:

1. Intelligence

2. Attractiveness (including both physical beauty and personal charisma)

3. Similarity

4. Physical proximity

5. High status

Most people I have polled choose either similarity, which is the correct answer, or attractiveness—which is another way of saying *similarity*, since the research also shows that we

A Network Audit

Think of up to ten people with whom you have discussed important work matters over the past few months (you are not required to come up with ten). You might have sought them out for advice, to bounce ideas off them, to help you evaluate opportunities, or to help you strategize important moves. Don't worry about who they should be. Only name people to whom you have actually turned for this help recently.

List their names or initials below, without reading further.

1. _____

2. _____

3. _____

4. _____

5. _____

6. _____

7. _____

8. _____

are more likely to be attracted to people with whom we have important things in common—and who therefore remind us of ourselves. Of course, we may be drawn to qualities like intelligence or status, but because we are talking about mutual attraction here, qualities like status and intelligence only create chemistry when both people are similar with respect to the qualities.

9. _____

10. _____

Take a moment to examine the names you listed. List up to three strengths and three weaknesses of having this set of connections at the core of your network:

The main strengths of my network as it exists today are:

1. _____

2. _____

3. _____

The main weaknesses of my network as it exists today are:

1. _____

2. _____

3. _____

We'll return to your answers later.

I call this tendency to prefer interacting with people who are similar to ourselves the *narcissistic principle* of relationship formation, and it is a very robust finding across decades of social science research.[3] We are drawn spontaneously to people who are like us in ways that are important to us, and we give those people the benefit of the doubt, creating conditions that increase the likelihood that a relationship will develop. The narcissistic principle is especially strong under conditions of threat or ambiguity, when we seek safety and certainty. Evolutionary psychologists explain this primitive instinct in terms of our prehistoric need to determine quickly whether a stranger is a potential friend or foe.[4] In those days, mistakes were very costly for our survival.

Some scholars argue that our tendency to use "like me" indicators to size up newcomers is hardwired and therefore still difficult to override today, even in a business world that thrives on diversity. A famous set of studies established, for example, that the success of an employment interview hinges on what transpires in the first few minutes of the encounter.[5] If both parties somehow establish some important common ground early on by noting, for example, that they share a hometown, an alma mater, or a common acquaintance, the chances that the interview will go well go up exponentially.

Without common ground, it's harder to relate to people. I see this every day at INSEAD, where I teach. Despite our rich international diversity in the classroom (and the obvious fact that just being there creates a lot of common ground), at lunch or dinner, people inevitably sit with their compatriots. In organizational life, we are likewise divided into our various "tribes"—people who share the same technical expertise, professional jargon, generational norms, national culture, educational background, career prospects, and so on. It takes more time and effort to get to know members of different tribes, which leads us to the second principle of relationship formation: the *lazy principle*.

After similarity, the second-most important determinant of chemistry in a relationship, according to the studies, is physical proximity.[6] Not only are we narcissistic, but we're also lazy. We get to know and like people who are easy to get to know and like because we bump into them with minimal effort. Just consider any organization that is spread across more than one building. Typically, few relationships survive the walk to the adjacent offices. Worse, people just hang out with others who occupy the same floor, most likely members of the same department or team. The same tendency exists outside work. One landmark study found that the likelihood of friendship among neighbors in an apartment block was significantly higher than the likelihood of friendship across blocks.[7] Most friendships were formed among people living on the same floor.

You can't possibly stay current with new trends in the world, much less lead the way, if your network is a product of the narcissistic and lazy bias. Unlike delivery-driven executives who network to do today's job, effective leaders create and use networks to tap new ideas, connect to people in different worlds, and access radically different perspectives. As we'll see, effective leaders have many people they can turn to who can help them think through difficult problems or support them in their initiatives. These leaders understand that the time spent building and maintaining their connections is an investment in their leadership skills. Because no one person can possibly have all the answers or, indeed, know all the right questions to ask, it's crucial that leaders be able to tap into a network of people who can fill in the gaps.

Acting like a leader, then, is not just about what you do, but also about the company you keep, as the sidebar "How Leaders Use Networks as an Essential Leadership Tool" summarizes. Stepping up to leadership, as we'll see below, requires that you cultivate a diverse, widespread, dynamic, and cross-cutting set of relationships to help you to lead change, move into assignments in which you can play a bigger leadership role, and take charge of your professional development.

How Leaders Use Networks as an Essential Leadership Tool

- Sensing trends and seeing opportunities

- Building ties to opinion leaders and talent in diverse areas

- Working collaboratively across boundaries to create more value

- Avoiding groupthink ⚡

- Generating breakthrough ideas

- Obtaining career opportunities

Mind-sets That Create Network Traps

Many managers like Robert (see chapter 2) limit both their capacity to lead and their career prospects because they end up sticking to the same old players for insight, perspective, and advice. As described earlier, Robert languished in the same staff role he had held for years. He felt increasingly bored and frustrated in a job he could have done "in his sleep." He was loyal to his company and to a boss who had given him opportunities in the past, but the boss didn't see Robert's leadership potential. Robert tried to break the impasse by enlisting other senior leaders in his firm to mentor him. These efforts were not getting him anywhere. Was he just too impatient, he wondered?

The introverted Robert didn't need more mentors. He sorely needed to broaden his horizons so that he could envision himself in a different capacity and show his superiors that their view of him was outdated. So against his natural inclinations, he eventually forced himself to start building relationships "outside the house."

He began by setting up lunches with former peers who had left the company for competitors or start-ups. He talked to headhunters and even began to chat with people at his health club to learn about their career trajectories. Robert's growing external network helped him get a bird's-eye view of his business and industry. It also gave him information on how other people had made transitions like the one he wanted to make. Robert's new relationships gave him a newfound appreciation of his own strengths and experience—an improved self-image that ultimately helped build his confidence.

Once he saw for himself the value of networking, Robert had no qualms about allocating time to it. Unfortunately, we don't invest in networking when we have a limited view of what it is really about, what it can do for us, and what we can do for others by virtue of the networks we've cultivated. For every manager who sees the value of maintaining a far-reaching and diverse set of connections, many more struggle to overcome innate resistance to, if not distaste for, networking.

Many of the managers I teach say that they find networking essentially insincere or manipulative—a way to obtain favors from strangers, with strings attached as obligations to return the favors. Carlos, a product manager for a consumer-goods firm, dismissed networking as "using people." For him, networking—the creation of a circle of personal contacts who can provide support, insight, information, and other resources— amounted to "lining people up for when I might need them." It was insincere and manipulative—at best, a sanctioned way of using people. As the sidebar "When Networking Makes You Feel Dirty" shows, he is not alone: many people report that

When Networking Makes You Feel Dirty[a]

Three business school professors, Tiziana Casciaro, Francesca Gino, and Maryam Kouchaki, decided to study something they had experienced personally and heard about often from their MBA students: people's strong distaste for "instrumental networking," which they defined as trying to make connections to advance one's career (as opposed to "personal networking," which is more spontaneous and aims to build friendly, collegial connections).

In two of their studies, even just thinking about instrumental networking made study subjects feel dirty, to the point that they thought unconsciously about taking a shower or brushing their teeth, or rated products associated with cleansing, such as Windex, Dove soap, and Crest toothpaste, as more desirable than neutral products, such as Post-it Notes and Nantucket Nectars juice.

To show they were onto something relevant outside the lab, Casciaro, Gino, and Kouchaki designed a third study, in which they surveyed lawyers at a large North American law firm. The authors found that the more power people have, the less likely they are to have qualms about instrumental networking. They asked the lawyers to fill out forms about the frequency of their networking activities, and then a questionnaire in which they had to complete the sentence, "When I engage in professional networking, I usually feel . . . ," followed by a choice of adjectives: "dirty," "ashamed," "inauthentic," "uncomfortable," or "happy," "excited," "anxious," "satisfied." The higher up they were in the firm, the less likely the lawyers were to select the negative adjectives.

In order to better tease out the effects of having power from the feelings associated with instrumental versus personal networking, the authors devised a fourth study in which they manipulated both the study subjects' level of power and the type of networking they were asked to do. Some participants were told they had a low-level position in their company, while others were told they had positions of power. Next, some participants were instructed to send a LinkedIn message aimed at building a professional relationship, while the others were asked to send a message through Facebook in order to develop a personal relationship. The authors then assessed the feelings of the participants and found that, overall, those who sent personal messages on Facebook felt a lot less dirty than those who sent professional messages on LinkedIn. However, the people who were told they held low-level positions chose more cleansing products when they sent the LinkedIn messages than those who were assigned power positions. The "higher-ups" didn't differ all that much in their product choice, whether they were sending Facebook or LinkedIn messages.

What did the authors conclude, knowing (from their own research and that of others) how important instrumental networks are for career success? They learned that confidence has a lot to do with an individual's comfort level with this kind of networking: the senior lawyers didn't feel conflicted about professional networking because they believed they had something of value to offer. The people in low-level positions, on the other hand, were more likely to doubt the worth of their contributions; they felt more like supplicants than peers in a reciprocal, mutually beneficial exchange.

a. Tiziana Casciaro, Francesca Gino, and Maryam Kouchaki, "The Contaminating Effects of Building Instrumental Ties: How Networking Can Make Us Feel Dirty." Harvard Business School Working Paper, No. 14-108, April 2014.

networking for instrumental purposes literally makes them feel unclean.

Because working the network felt like a threat to his integrity, Carlos stayed inside his comfort zone, which was defined by his long-standing relationships within his region's operations. He had excellent local networks; a natural extrovert, Carlos also took advantage of extracurricular activities like golf outings at his club to strengthen his relationships with customers, team members, and even colleagues outside his group. But having spent the totality of his career in his home country of Brazil, he lacked the strategic ties that his highly mobile, often expatriated peers enjoyed. What he most needed now was visibility with decision makers, the people who sat at the table for promotion decisions. "I know there are people I need to stay in touch with, strategically," he said. "But I have always been in Brazil, so I struggle to keep contact with people who aren't based here. What am I supposed to do, send an email saying, 'How's it going?'? That seems fake to me. I feel more comfortable saying, 'Let's talk about the business.' I know I have to work on this, but it's not easy."

Like Carlos, many people who fail to engage in networking justify their choice as a matter of personal values. Jacob, whom we saw in chapter 1 struggling to carve out quiet time for strategizing about his business, also told me that his distaste for instrumental behavior was holding him back from building the relationships he needed: "Relationships should develop in a natural way." Furthermore, his career path within a large, well-organized multinational had not prepared him for networking across boundaries: "My firm was like a cocoon: Everything was organized—it's a world in which you don't need an external network. Even the management courses were internal—bringing together company people from all around the world." His limited interactions made it difficult for him to fully appreciate the demands on sales, finance, and other functional areas, so he could hardly blend these diverse perspectives into a viable business strategy, no matter how much time he spent shut up in his office.

As people step up to leadership, some accept their growing dependence on others and seek to transform it into mutual influence. Others dismiss such work as political and, as a result, undermine their ability to advance their goals. As we saw in chapter 2, recruiting stakeholders, lining up allies and sympathizers, and sensing the political landscape are all part of the leader's job. When we define networking as intrinsically self-interested, even somewhat sleazy—and who among us wants to define ourselves in those terms?—we will always prioritize immediate tasks and personal relationships over longer-term strategic network investments that may or may not pay off in the future. The only way to conceive of networking in nobler, more appealing ways is to do it, and experience for ourselves its value, not only for ourselves but also for our teams and organizations.

A lack of experience with networking also leads people to question whether it's a legitimate use of their time, especially when the relationships being developed are not immediately related to the task at hand. When we don't consider networking an integral part of our job and professional responsibilities, we understandably find this activity hard to squeeze in. Why widen our circle of acquaintances speculatively, when there is hardly enough time for the real work? The sidebar "Traps That Keep You from Expanding Your Networks" summarizes the objections that many of us have about networks.

Traps like these create powerful network blinders. They make you more vulnerable to the narcissistic and lazy syndrome that

Traps That Keep You from Expanding Your Networks

- You think networking is not real work.

- You think it is using people and it feels inauthentic.

- The payoff is long term, and you have more urgent things to do.

- You think that relationships should form spontaneously.

narrows your thinking and limits your capacity to lead. You remain inside a cozy but closed circle that leaves you and your team vulnerable to shifting winds and unprepared to anticipate them. Worse, you reduce your utility to the people who rely on you as a contact, because you have little to offer that they don't know already (or can't get elsewhere). Moving past these traps takes knowledge of how different kinds of networks work.

Operational, Personal, and Strategic Networks

Of course, you already have a network. The question is what kind.

At least three different networks—*operational*, *personal*, and *strategic*—can play a vital role in helping you step up to lead. The first helps you manage current internal responsibilities, the second boosts personal development, and the third focuses on new business directions and the stakeholders you must get on board to pursue these directions. While people differ a lot in how well they build and use operational and personal networks, I discovered that nearly everyone underutilizes strategic networking. Let me briefly describe each type of network (table 3-1).

Most of the people I come across have good *operational networks*. These networks include the people on whom you depend in order to get your work done. The people include your direct reports, your superiors, people in other units, and key outsiders such as suppliers, distributors, and customers. The composition of your networks is largely determined by your immediate job needs and routine, short-term demands. Of course, it is up to you to deepen, develop, and prioritize the relationships that are most important for you. But you have little discretion in the composition of operational networks, because these tend to be prescribed by the job and organizational structure. A good operational network gives you *reliability*. But it's unlikely to deliver value beyond helping you accomplish functional objectives and assigned tasks. The network won't help you ask the strategic and future-focused question "What should we be doing instead?"

Most people also have *personal networks* of varying diversity and breadth. Here you have lots of discretion about who's in. Personal networks include relationships with the people that you feel closest to—friends, family, and trusted advisers—and the

TABLE 3-1

Difference between operational, personal, and strategic networks

	Operational network	Personal network	Strategic network
Purpose	Manage today's work; get things done efficiently	Grow personally and professionally; enjoy and develop yourself	Lead: understand your context, generate strategic ideas, and get support for them
Location and time frame	Mostly internal; short-term focus	Mostly external; short- and medium-term focus	Both internal and external; medium- and long-term focus
Key relationships	Nondiscretionary; key contacts are mostly prescribed by the task and organizational structure	Discretionary; key contacts are driven by current interests and immediate career priorities	Some discretion but strategic relevance matters; key contacts are defined by the industry and organizational environment

people you meet through things like professional associations, alumni groups, clubs, hobbies, charities, and other personal-interest communities. You decide who belongs in this network according to your personal goals and affinities. A good personal network gives you *kindred spirits*. It can also provide important referrals, widen your professional involvement and horizons outside work, and, in the best cases, offer developmental support such as coaching or mentoring. When you are looking for a new job or career advice, you typically start with this network.

But personal networking absorbs a significant amount of time and energy. This is one reason that many people stop networking, precisely when they need it most—when they are busy delivering on routine work (and pick it back up when they desperately need a new job). They see their personal circle as something totally divorced from their day-to-day work, instead of looking for potential synergies between their operational and personal contacts so that each circle enriches and strengthens the other.

The third kind of network—your *strategic network*—is made up of relationships that help you to envision the future, sell your ideas, and get the information and resources you need to exploit these ideas. It requires both time and attention outside operational demands and strategic investment in outside activities that can give you outsight on what else you might be doing. You have more discretion about the composition of your strategic network than you do in your operational network, but not as much as in your personal network. By definition, a strategic network has to include people and groups that can help you compete in the future. Part of the trick is that it is not always so obvious who should be a part of this network. A good strategic network gives you *connective advantage*: the ability to marshal information, support, or other resources from one of your networks to obtain results in another. It's not so much about the one-on-one relationships you have, but it is more about how they intersect.

As we'll see, there are three basic sources of connective advantage that you will need to build into your network. As you read the next section, you may want to return to the network audit that you took at the beginning of this chapter, to assess if these properties of networks are working for you or against you.

The BCDs (Breadth, Connectivity, and Dynamism) of Networking Advantage

Your network's strategic advantage and, therefore, the extent to which it helps you step up to leadership, depends on three qualities:

- **Breadth:** Strong relationships with a diverse range of contacts

- **Connectivity:** The capacity to link or bridge across people and groups that wouldn't otherwise connect

- **Dynamism:** A dynamic set of extended ties that evolves as you evolve)

I call these three qualities the BCDs of network advantage, or $A = B + C + D$.

Breadth: How Diverse Is Your Network?

One of the first things that my students notice when they audit their networks is that the network formed by the people they talk to about important work matters is much more internally focused than it should be. As these managers start to concern themselves with broad strategic issues and organizational change processes, lateral relationships with people outside their immediate area become even more critical to the managers' ability to get things done. And in a connected world, building stronger external networks to tap into the best sources of insight into environmental trends is also part and parcel of the leadership role.

Data compiled from the network surveys I give my participants shows that we are still not using networks to our best advantage. We build networks that are heavily skewed toward our own functional, business, or geographical group and fail to elicit or value the input and perspectives of peers from different functional or support groups. Moreover, we are still relying on networks that are mostly internal to our company, in a world where the rate of change outside is considerable. ✒

As the descriptive statistics in figure 3-2 show, the majority of my students' contacts are inside their specialty, unit, and firm. On average, less than 43 percent of the people the executive students were discussing key issues with were located outside their unit or specialty; even fewer, only a quarter, were external to their company. But averages can be deceiving: the range of values shows that some of the managers in the survey have no outsight at all from their networks, with no contacts at all outside their specialty, unit, or firm.

You can also overdo diversity: the ranges also show that some of the executives have heavily external networks: up to 100 percent and 95 percent outside their specialties and units, respectively, and 88 percent outside their companies. That's fine if an executive is looking to move elsewhere, as some of my participants were. But an exclusively outside network is not as useful if you are trying to bring an outside approach into your own company. As we learned in chapter 2, you can't bridge the outside to the inside if you haven't established strong relationships on the inside.

FIGURE 3-2

Network diversity: external focus

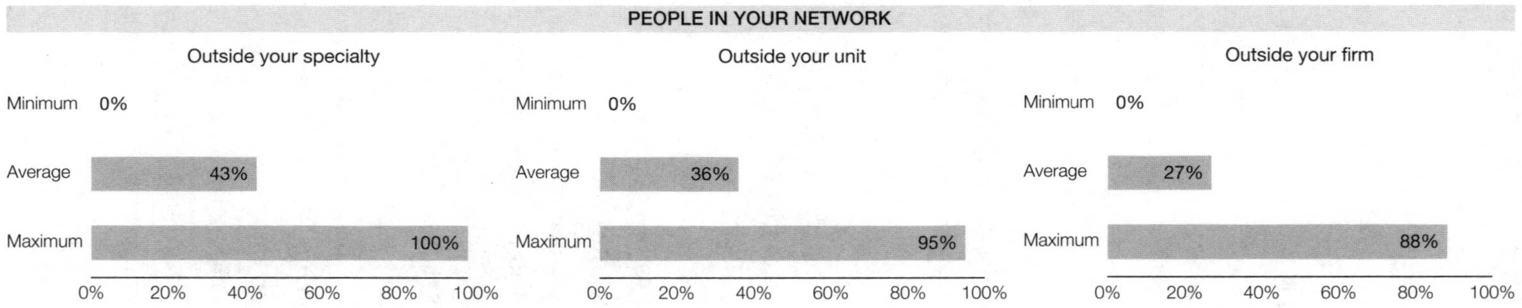

PEOPLE IN YOUR NETWORK
Outside your specialty
Minimum
0%
Average
43%
Maximum
100%
0%
20%
40%
60%
80%
100%
Outside your unit
Minimum
0%
Average
36%
Maximum
95%
0%
20%
40%
60%
80%
100%
Outside your firm
Minimum
0%
Average
27%
Maximum
88%
0%
20%
40%
60%
80%
100%

Source: Author's 2011–14 survey of 156 alumni from INSEAD executive programs.

Another common network blind spot consists of undervaluing the potential contributions of junior people. Managers striving to make their way up the leadership pipeline tend to manage up, forgetting that their connection to the layers below is often what makes them invaluable to seniors whose sponsorship they hope to attract. One manager explained it to me this way: "I would perhaps have been able to add even more value to my superiors if I had retained my links with more junior people. For example, recently we were in a meeting discussing the results of a global people survey. I was listening to all their comments, and I said, 'You guys are looking at this from the perspective of very senior people; be careful about how you are interpreting the results. [People at a lower level] are saying something completely different.' I knew that because I had been spending time with them." Given a choice between a network heavily skewed to the power players in your firm and a good mix of diverse contacts, which would you choose? Research shows that you are better off with the latter. This is because networks run on the principle of *reciprocity.* The value of diverse relationships lies not only in what your contacts can do for you, but also on what you can do for them. Your senior leaders don't need you to connect them with other seniors; they already know each other. Top management needs you to bring them the fresh ideas, insights, and best practices that you can only get elsewhere, outside, across, and below. As figure 3-3 shows, too many managers lack the 360-degree perspective you can only get from cultivating relationships with a mix of peers, juniors, and seniors. Although the averages suggest that people focus their networking on approximately one-third of each group, the range of the scores shows that too many managers systematically exclude one of these groups. The sidebar "Why We Need Fresh Blood" explains how diversity on any team often produces the best results.

FIGURE 3-3

Network diversity: across levels

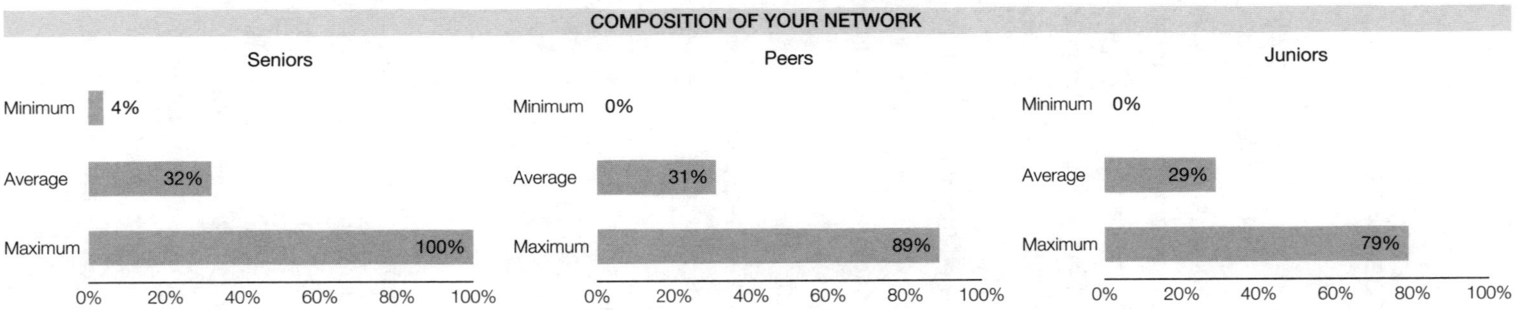

COMPOSITION OF YOUR NETWORK

Seniors

Minimum	4%
Average	32%
Maximum	100%

Peers

Minimum	0%
Average	31%
Maximum	89%

Juniors

Minimum	0%
Average	29%
Maximum	79%

Source: Author's 2011–14 survey of 156 alumni from INSEAD executive programs.

Why We Need Fresh Blood

Stefan Wuchty, Benjamin Jones, and Brian Uzzi, a multidisciplinary team of researchers, decided to use big data to learn what distinguished ideas that had impact from those that didn't. In a massive study of the twenty million academic articles and two million patents cited over the past fifty years, which Wuchty and his colleagues published in the prestigious journal *Science,* they found that the difference lies in the kinds of networks that produce the ideas.[a]

The study showed that the days of the solitary genius or lone inventor—think Newton or Einstein—are over. Creative and scientific work has migrated to teams and, more recently, to large, distributed teams like the hundreds of scientists that worked on the human genome project.

But being part of a team wasn't enough for high impact, as measured by article and patent citations. The really great ideas were much more likely to come from cross-institutional collaborations rather than from teams from the same university, lab, or research center. Not only that, but the most successful

On making a list of their relationships, even highly experienced leaders find that they've been narcissistic and lazy, failing to network with people who are different from them or to build bridges across and outside their organization's lines. Check the diversity of your network by returning to the list you made at the beginning of this chapter. To what extent are your relationships externally facing? Have you included a good mix of people occupying different levels and functions?

teams mixed things up. They avoided the trap of always work-ing with the same people, and successful groups brought to the team both newcomers and people who had never collabo-rated before.

Uzzi and another colleague, Jarrett Spiro, also discovered that this pattern held across sectors as disparate as the Broadway mu-sical industry and biotechnology.[b] Between 1920 and 1930, for example, 87 percent of Broadway shows flopped despite being attached to big names like Rogers and Hammerstein, or Gilbert and Sullivan. When well-known composers like these continued to work together without the benefit of fresh blood, their creations suffered, critically and financially. The most successful plays, in-stead, resulted from collaborations among diverse players. Leon-ard Bernstein's *West Side Story*, for example, which went on to become a megahit, featured newcomer Stephen Sondheim and other new collaborators.

a. Stefan Wuchty, Benjamin F. Jones, and Brian Uzzi, "The Increasing Dominance of Teams in Production of Knowledge," *Science* 316, no. 5827 (2007): 1036–1039.

b. Brian Uzzi and Jarrett Spiro, "Collaboration and Creativity: The Small World Problem," *American Journal of Sociology* 111, no. 2 (2005): 447–504.

How Connective Is Your Network?

So far we've looked at who the people are in your network and how you are connected to these people. Now we'll turn to how your contacts are connected and what that means for you.

The connectivity of your network is the basis for the famous *six degrees of separation* principle—the idea that we are rarely ever more than six links removed from anyone else in world through the friends of our friends—discovered by Harvard psychologist

Stanley Milgram in the 1960s.[8] As any LinkedIn user knows, the fewer degrees of separation between any two people in a network, the easier it is to access the resources you need.

In the original study, Milgram gave a bunch of people in Nebraska a letter destined for a stockbroker in Massachusetts—a man they didn't know. Their job was to get the letter to him by sending it to someone they did know, who might then send it to someone else, ultimately reaching the stockbroker. Milgram found that it never took more than six links (thus the six-degrees concept) to reach the stockbroker, for those letters that actually arrived. But many of the letters never got there, because the first degree—the people his participants knew directly and contacted first—didn't have networks that reached outside their local environment. So, many of the letters never got out of Nebraska. They only circulated inside the same circle of people who all knew each other.

Something similar happens when you fall prey to the narcissistic and lazy trap in your networking: everyone you know knows the same people you do, and the flow of information gets stuck in the same office, in the same industry, in the same neighborhood. Sociologists use the term *density* to describe this property of networks: it quantifies the percentage of people who know each other in a network. Density is an imperfect measure, but it is a quick way to check how much six-degree potential you have in your network. See the sidebar "Calculate Your Network's Density."

Calculate Your Network's Density

Go back to the list of up to ten contacts you made at the start of this chapter, and put their names in the grid provided here.

Using only the *unshaded* portion of the grid, place a checkmark to indicate which pairs of people know each other. If you are not sure whether two people know each other, assume they don't.

Start with person 1, and run along the top row checking if person 1 knows persons 2, 3, 4, and so on. Then go to person 2, and do the same until you have considered all the people on your list.

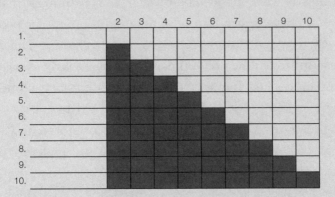

Now, compute the density of your network following these steps:

1. Count the total number of people on your list (the maximum is 10), and write it down here: _____

2. Take that number, and multiply it by the number minus 1. Then divide the result by 2, and write it down here: _____

3. Count the total number of checkmarks on your grid (i.e., the number of links that exist between the various people on your list), and write that number here: _____

4. Take the number you obtained in step 3, and divide it by the number you got in step 2. This is the density of your network. Write it here: _____

The lower your network's density score, the less inbred your network (note that lower isn't necessarily better because too low a density, as I explain below, can be problematic too).

If you are like many of the successful executives I teach, chances are that your density score is higher than it should be. When I conduct this exercise in class, the average density hovers above 50 percent, although it is significantly lower for professionals who work mostly with outside clients such as consultants, investment bankers, lawyers, headhunters, and auditors and for people who go back to school to orchestrate a career change. The range of scores always extends to 100 percent: when nearly everyone with whom you discuss important work issues knows each other, you have an inbred network. There's no other way to put it.

To understand the problems of having an inbred network, let's look at the effects of network density in a completely different context: the so-called obesity epidemic. Two previously unknown university professors, Nicholas Christakis and James Fowler, became overnight celebrities when they showed that being overweight can be contagious.[9]

Christakis and Fowler analyzed the health records and social relationships of twelve thousand Framingham, Massachusetts, residents from 1948 to the present. Using advanced visualization techniques and careful statistical controls, they showed that overweight people tend to hang together socially, while thin people tend to be friends with other thin people. But this is not a mere correlation showing that birds of a feather flock together: being connected socially to people who are overweight, even indirectly, seems to make a person overweight. The researchers concluded that thin and overweight people tend to live their lives within different and unconnected social clusters—"microclimates," so to speak— within which different social norms about what is normal and desirable have developed. Political views also hang by cluster. Tightly connected members apparently had no external perspective on the world beyond their immediate group.

At work, when we surround ourselves with people like us and with whom we've worked before, the network creates an echo chamber in which no new information circulates because everyone has the same sources. That's how groups become mired in consensus, and after a while, everyone thinks and acts alike. The sidebar "The Innovator's Network Dilemma" presents convincing data that bears out this observation.

The Innovator's Network Dilemma

A study by University of Chicago sociologist Ron Burt demonstrates the cost of inbred networks.

When Burt studied managers in the supply chain of Raytheon, the large electronics company and military contractor based in Waltham, Massachusetts, he discovered that the company had no trouble coming up with good ideas but considerable difficulty turning these ideas into reality.

Burt asked the managers to write down their best ideas about how to improve business operations, and then he asked two executives at the company to rate the quality of these ideas. He then mapped out the network of who consulted with whom. Burt was looking for what he calls "structural holes," gaps between cohesive groups of people with dense patterns of informal communication among them and few ties outside their circle.

His many years of research have shown that people whose networks span these holes reap the greatest network benefits. These people see more and know more. They have more power because other people have to go through them to connect outside their group.

> Not surprisingly, the highest-ranked ideas came from managers who had contacts outside their immediate work group. Most managers, however, overwhelmingly turned to colleagues already close in their informal discussion network to bounce ideas off (think "inbred circle"). The result was that their ideas were not developed.[a]
>
> a. Ronald S. Burt, *Structural Holes: The Social Structure of Competition* (Cambridge, MA: Harvard University Press, 1995); Ronald S. Burt, "Structural Holes and Good Ideas," *American Journal of Sociology* 110, no. 2 (2004): 349–399. See also Gautam Ahuja, "Collaboration Networks, Structural Holes, and Innovation: A Longitudinal Study," *Administrative Science Quarterly* 45, no. 3 (2000): 425–455.

This state of affairs also limits significantly how valuable you are to your network, since you bring nothing unique that the network members can't get elsewhere. Your comparative advantage—how you differentiate yourself from others who are as smart, hardworking, or expert as you are—depends on your capacity to connect people, ideas, and resources that wouldn't normally bump into one another.

Some research suggests that there's an optimum level of density, about 40 percent.[10] But of course, that depends a lot on what a person's job is. When your network gets too sparse, you lose connectivity. You are a "visitor" to many networks but a "citizen" of none. You may have access to lots of ideas and people, but you can't put them to use inside your organization (or any other group to which you belong), because you lack inside information about how to pitch your ideas, who might be opposed to them, and how to win people over—all critical parts of leading change (as discussed in chapter 2).[11]

Too sparse a network, and you might also lack credibility and visibility with important gatekeepers, who might not know you well but who implicitly evaluate you on the basis of who you know that they also know (the principle on which professional networks like LinkedIn work). This is often a problem when you are the minority in a group. As described earlier, the narcissistic and lazy principle holds that people are apt to have relationships with people like them, so minorities and majorities and professional men and women are unlikely to have highly overlapping networks.[12] In a study of boards of directors, for example, James Westphal found that minority directors tend to be more influential if they have direct or indirect social network ties to majority directors through common memberships on other boards.[13] These overlapping networks serve as a form of social verification and increase the likelihood that the minority's ideas will be heard.

In sum, as Malcolm Gladwell illustrated in his book *The Tipping Point*, networks run on "connectors," people who are linked to almost everyone else in a few steps and who connect the rest of us to the world.[14] Connectors can see a need in one place and a solution in another, a vacancy in one area and a talented person in another, a discovery from a different discipline and a problem in their own, and so on, because they're just one or two "chain lengths" away from the issues. That is, you can reach connectors through someone you already know or through someone who knows someone whom you already know.

How Dynamic Is Your Network?

One of the biggest drawbacks of a narcissistic and lazy network is that it quickly becomes a historical artifact, the residue of manager's past rather than a tool to move into the future. We change jobs, firms, and even countries, but our networks lag behind our new responsibilities and aspirations and therefore pigeonhole us just when we need a fresh perspective or seek to move into something different. Joel Podolny, former head of Apple's human resources, calls this tendency of our networks to evolve more slowly than our jobs "network lag."[15] We're exceptionally slow to build relationships that allow us to perform in a new position or prepare us for future roles.

When asked about the strengths of their network, most people think first about the *quality* of their relationships. They value most their strong ties, because trust is essential when it comes to getting things done, and we trust most the people we know best. But as we have seen, the people we know best are not necessarily those who can prepare us for stepping up. To make your networks future facing, you'll need to build and value your weak ties—that is, the people and groups that are currently on the periphery of your network, those you don't see very often or don't know so well (see the sidebar "Making a Network Future Facing").[16] What's important about these contacts is not the quality of your relationship with them (just yet), but the fact that they come from outside your current world. These contacts tend to be several levels removed from you or circulate in different circles.

That makes reaching out harder. Getting to know your weak ties or getting to know them better usually requires an explicit plan and strategy—these relationships will never evolve naturally, because you have no common context in which to develop them. Nevertheless, these are the ties from which you stand to gain the greatest outsight.

Another problem with relying exclusively on your strong-tie network is that it limits your capacity to rethink yourself (the topic of chapter 4). In my study of thirty-nine midcareer managers and professionals considering major career changes, I observed directly how much their old networks can "bind and blind" them. All of them were told by a friend, family member, or close coworker that they must be out of their minds for thinking about quitting their jobs or leaving their organizations. The people close to you may mean well, but they are often not helpful when you are

Making a Network Future Facing

A financial services firm executive, Pam, realized that she was unprepared when her job became more externally facing. "I was fairly well networked internally and within my region," she told me, "but I had no external network or external points of connectivity, and I don't think I understood the value of those external points." Never one to give much thought to whom she knew, she realized the time had come to build a new network systematically. Here are the steps she followed:

- Identify twenty to twenty-five key stakeholders you wish to stay connected to in a meaningful way.

- Assign these contacts into key categories:

    - Most-senior clients

    - Most-senior people in your company

    - Most-senior hedge fund people and competitors

    - Most-senior service providers (e.g., lawyers, accountants)

    - Most-senior women in financial services

- For each category, select the three to five people you want to stay connected to.

- Decide how frequently you will reach out to each contact.

trying to stretch yourself. Despite their good intentions, they hold restrictive views of who you are and what you can do. So, they are the people most likely to reinforce—or even desperately try to preserve—the old identity you are trying to shed.

Do you remember Robert's story? Recall that his goal of moving into a general management role in his company remained a pipe dream as long as his mentors within the company held on to an outdated image of his capacity. He had access to the power center of his firm, but was unsure about himself—whether he had sufficient expertise to seize the helm of a business unit successfully. The people around him, who also doubted that he was ready to take the leap, amplified his lack of self-confidence. The same might also hold for you: it can be difficult to get support for change from old mentors, bosses, or trusted colleagues whose views on you are based on the past and not the future. That's yet one more reason to refresh your network, so that it also grows with you.

What's Wrong with Your Network?

Return to the network audit that you completed at the beginning of this chapter, and check what you listed as the strengths and weaknesses of your current network. Which of the following weaknesses that we discussed above are true for you?

- **Birds of a feather:** Your contacts are too homogeneous, all like you.

- **Network lag:** Your network is about your past, not your future.

- **Echo chamber:** Your contacts are all internal; they all know each other.

- **Pigeonholing:** Your contacts can't see you doing something different.

These three sources of network advantage—the diversity of your contacts, your connectivity within the network, and your network's dynamism—are obviously interrelated. Without these advantages, you never meet new people and the circle closes; over time, you lose outsight and relevance. The rest of this chapter explains some simple steps for breaking out of these blinders, which I summarize in the sidebar "What's Wrong with Your Network?"

How to Network Out and Across

Thinking like a leader starts by acting on your network. Start on the periphery of your current network, and build outward by getting involved in new activities, asking the people you already know to connect you with others, doing some maintenance, and finding kindred spirits who are also working to step up.

Show Up

Woody Allen's famous quip that "80 percent of success is showing up" is a great guide to expanding your network. (Of course, he also added, "Sometimes it's easier to hide home in bed. I've done both.")

As we saw in chapter 2, managers can start expanding their jobs by building on their interests or domains of expertise through professional associations, industry groups, alumni networks, and the like. All of these important sources of outsight also provide ready-made networks to which you can easily connect to share and multiply your knowledge. Communities of practice exist (or can easily be created on the internet) in almost every area of business you might be interested in, from brand management to private equity to product innovation, to cite just a few examples.[17] Sign up and show up.

But that is only the first step. If you stop there, you are only building your personal network. To make these connections strategic, savvy managers use what they are gleaning outside the boundaries of their jobs and companies as a hook for making valuable internal connections to previously untapped people and groups, setting the stage for addressing strategic concerns.

Many of the successful networkers I've met leverage their personal interests to create their own communities. For example, an investment banker who specialized in the tech sector started inviting key clients to the theater (a passion of hers) several times a year as a way of making sure she saw the plays she wanted to see. She had her assistant buy a block of tickets and organize a fast buffet dinner before the play at a hotel near the theater district. Over time, she and her clients started bringing other members of the local high-tech community to her events. Because a lot of business was done at the dinners, they attracted even more of the relevant people to future events. The group eventually became too big for her budget, but none of the attendees minded paying their own way, because they got so much out of it. Through these events, the investment banker developed her own business, and the knowledge she gained about her clients' companies generated business and ideas for other divisions in her firm.

The investment banker's experience clearly illustrates how our own personal interests can expand our networks. The sidebar "Invest in Activities That Will Grow Your Network" lists several possible routes down this path.

As you get used to showing up, you should then consider the importance of speaking up. This is a corollary that I learned from my own experience. I found that I wasn't getting as much as I'd

Invest in Activities That Will Grow Your Network

- Use projects and assignments strategically.

- Invest in extracurricular activities.

- Create your own communities of interest.

- Use lunches and business trips to connect to people you don't see often.

- Favor active rather than passive networking opportunities (for example, don't just show up for events—organize, or speak at them).

- Use social media to broadcast your interests and cast a wider net to people who share them.

like out of the many conferences and other events I was attending. So, I came up with a principle: Today, I won't attend unless I am speaking or at least introducing the speakers or moderating a panel (of course, I make exceptions to this rule).

I realize that this is easy enough advice for me to give after twenty-five years of public speaking. But when you speak up in front of a group, people learn enough about you to decide if they want to learn more. In the networking that follows, they already know who you are. All this interaction increases the likelihood that your time investment will be worthwhile. In my case, when I'm not actively involved, I tend to arrive too late for the pre-networking, I multitask on my phone during the talk (because I'm busy and there is always something urgent to handle at home or at work), and I quickly exit after the formal part of the event, forgoing the real reason everyone is there—to connect informally. It's not surprising that I wasn't getting much out of these events.

Anyone can start by organizing a panel, presenting a speaker, or moderating the question-and-answer session. You can even start by just posing a well-formulated question to the panel or speaker, provided you state clearly your name and what you do. After you've followed these suggestions a few times, it won't take you much longer to be more involved than it would just to attend the conference. But the payoff in your networking will be huge in comparison. One young woman I spoke to, a digital strategy expert who had built her own consulting and speaking business, explained that she never tries to network before she speaks at a conference. Most people assume that her youth makes her irrelevant to them. After the talk, she told me, they are not paying attention to her age anymore—they know she has relevant information for them. So don't just show up; take whatever chance you can to speak up.

Use Your Two Degrees of Separation

Like so many of Milgram's participants in the six-degrees experiment, many of us still have trouble getting outside Nebraska. But the world has become much smaller since Milgram's day. More recent findings show that in today's hyperconnected world, we can link to almost anyone else in just slightly over four degrees.[18]

Within any given professional domain, our connections are rarely more than two, at most three, degrees away as the "Oracle of Bacon" shows.[19] Type in the name of any actor you can think of, from any genre or country, from Bollywood to the new wave of Iranian films, and the Oracle will tell you how many degrees away that actor is from Kevin Bacon. For example, if you type in French actress Isabelle Adjani, you get a Bacon factor of two, because she acted in a film with Bill Bailey II, who in turn acted with Kevin Bacon in the 1995 film *Balto*. It's hard to get to three degrees, even when you put in an actor from the very early days of cinema, like Charlie Chaplin (two degrees away). That's why Reid Hoffman, LinkedIn's founder, finds that when it comes to meeting people who can help you professionally, three degrees of separation is as far as you can go. But we don't make good use of this connectivity, because most of us don't realize just how big and powerful our networks really are.[20]

I realized this point when I was asked to organize a strategic networking seminar that was offered as an elective for anyone in the top two hundred of a US *Fortune* 100 company that wanted to encourage its managers to develop a more external orientation. As part of the seminar, which was held in Paris, I organized a "six-degrees-of-separation dinner." I asked managers to use their networks to invite someone they had never met to the dinner. Most of the participants didn't reach past the first degree of separation, asking a friend or a colleague in France to suggest a possible guest.

It was a diverse group, but it wasn't very relevant. The next day's session included a discussion of disruptive trends in their businesses. I asked my managers how many of them had taken their own strategic concerns into account in deciding whom to invite. None of them had.

Good networkers are aware of and use their degrees of separation, reaching out regularly to their contacts' contacts and even to their third degree. Great networkers decrease the degrees of separation between their contacts and people they don't know but who might be useful to them. They add value by enlarging others' networks. Former Silicon Valley venture capitalist Heidi Roizen is a good example of one way to do this. Leveraging her love of entertaining, she made her San Francisco home a networking hub with her famous spaghetti dinners. The rule for these events was that half the people invited should not already know the other half. In a short time, her dinners became the hot ticket in town, a technique that Facebook's Sheryl Sandberg has become known for more recently.[21] The sidebar "Use Your Existing Connections to Branch Out" offers further suggestions for broadening your strategic network.

Do Some Maintenance

As his stint running the Taiwanese market for the Swiss food group Nestlé was coming to an end, Chris Johnson was put in charge of overseeing the global implementation of a new enterprise software system.[22] A line manager for most of his career, Chris had zero experience in IT. From his own experience running a profit-and-loss operation, he knew how much resistance he would get from his own peers, who would have to bear the cost of the new system while waiting patiently for it to pay off years later (in many cases after their own stints would be long

Use Your Existing Connections to Branch Out

- Ask for referrals and introductions; make them for others.

- Ask for simple favors to initiate a relationship.

- Do your homework before you reach out to someone new.

- Do the trite stuff—write thank you notes; forward links to articles; follow up using social media.

- Help your contacts develop their networks.

over). A previous effort had failed. The new plan was ambitious in terms of time and budget.

Chris's boss, the company's chief financial officer, helpfully suggested about a dozen names of people to start up the effort. Chris had no idea how to staff his team, because everything about the assignment was new to him. So, he reached out to his extensive network inside the company to get some help evaluating his boss's talent suggestions. Chris's contacts used their own networks to check out the people they themselves didn't know. The verdict that came back was not what Chris wanted to hear: most of the names the boss had suggested did not have credibility with the market heads, the people whose buy-in Chris most needed to succeed. Confident in the knowledge that the boss's suggestions were the wrong people for the job, Chris stood firm against his boss's wishes and bet his career on choosing his own people. Chris's stand was one of a few key decisions to which he attributed his ultimate success. Of course, he mobilized the same network to find the right talent to staff up the project.

Having a network that can turn on a dime as Chris's group did (his aggressive timeline gave him only a couple of weeks to staff up) requires some work on your part to keep it alive. Don't wait until you really need something badly to reach out. Instead, take every opportunity to nurture your network, whether you need it now or not.

Pam, the aforementioned financial services executive, reminded herself regularly to follow up with key people in her network. "I am expending effort on keeping my network alive," she said. "You can so easily get consumed in your day-to-day work that you forget that having lunch with certain people at least three times a year is really important. If you don't, you lose connectivity, and if you lose connectivity, you lose the relationship. I sort of said to myself, 'OK, so how frequently should I be tapping into these people?' I decided that some were twice a year; others might require monthly contact. I literally wrote emails to myself on a quarterly basis, asking, 'How am I doing?'"

Find Kindred Spirits

The fastest way to change yourself is to spend time with people who are already the way you want to be.[23] As we saw from the obesity study, the people you hang out with shape who you are and who you become. Behavior and the beliefs behind it are contagious: you can easily catch them, for better or for worse. If you spend your time with other leaders, chances are that you will become a leader, too.

Bill Wilson, the founder of Alcoholics Anonymous (AA), built his organization on this insight. He realized that successful change does not take as much willpower as it takes fellowship.[24] The key to success at AA is the daily group meeting in which old-timers who have managed to remain sober share their stories and mentor newcomers. The more time that members spend with other members, the more likely they all will remain sober. That's because recovering alcoholics don't just change their drinking behavior. They change the reference by which they judge what is possible and desirable.

Wilson's insight is supported by research in psychology on the power of reference groups.[25] It shows that whether we realize it or not, answers to the question "How well am I doing?" or "Am I on track?" are inherently comparative. We believe ourselves to be rich or poor, talented or average, strong or weak by comparison with others around us. Witness people's reactions to how much they are paid relative to their peer groups, or the bonding that happens in groups that, like the Young Presidents Organization, bring together people who share common concerns. The danger, of course, is that we can continue to compare ourselves against benchmarks that have lost their relevance, as Robert did, when he only compared his curriculum vitae to that of the other people who had chosen to stay in his company.

Reference groups composed of kindred spirits take on even greater importance in times of uncertainty such as when we are stepping up to leadership. When asked to do things that don't come naturally—working more collaboratively, for example—we implicitly ask ourselves, "Am I the sort of person who behaves this way?" and "Do I want to be that sort of person?" Stepping up to a bigger leadership role, just like becoming a nondrinker, thus requires a new point of reference.

New peer groups might consist of people who are experiencing similar challenges and doubts. Dieter, a new general manager, for example, struggled with all the usual transition hurdles—not delegating enough, not soliciting input but rather imposing his views impatiently on others. He knew, intellectually, that his new role required a shift away from the routine work he had done successfully before. "But at the same time," he said, "I worried about being seen as the one who does nothing himself." But who would actually see him that way? The other people in his company who were still stuck doing instead of leading. The conversations he had in a coaching group with other managers also striving to step up to leadership not only showed him that his concern was normal but also started to shift his reference group from his coworkers to people with goals similar to his.

Alternatively, people who have already made the kind of transition that you are contemplating can also serve as important guideposts. Take, for example, Andrew, a molecular biologist who worked on the faculty of a major research university. The academic peer group against which he had always measured himself disdained commercial activity. But Andrew had become intrigued by the possibility of leading teams in an effort to commercialize scientific discoveries. When one of his collaborators left academia,

Andrew stayed in touch and, through this person, got to know a new circle of scientists who had more positive views of commercial work. Over time, Andrew came to feel greater kinship with this circle of colleagues than with his old circle at the university. When he was offered the possibility of directing a major new center to foster partnerships between academia and commercial science, Andrew accepted.

Sustaining regular social contact with people who are in the same boat or have already arrived on the other side is essential for enduring change, because they can endorse and model your own transition to leadership. As you attain senior levels and broader responsibilities, you are easily isolated from these kinds of collegial and peer relationships. For this reason, you usually need to build these relationships outside the scope of your job and company.

Cultivate a Connected Mind

Riffing on Pasteur's famous dictum that "chance favors the prepared mind," Steven Johnson, innovation historian and author of *Where Good Ideas Come From*, concludes that "chance favors the connected mind."[26] Examining the creative process of legendary innovators like Benjamin Franklin and Charles Darwin, Johnson found that behind every great thinker, there is a diverse, connected, and dynamic network. "This is not the wisdom of the crowd," he says, "but the wisdom of someone in the crowd. It's not that the network itself is smart; it's that individuals get smarter because they're connected to the network."

As we have seen, when aspiring leaders fail to recognize networking as one of the most important requirements of their new job, they will not allocate enough time and effort to networking to see it pay off. But the only way to understand that networking is a key source of outsight for your leadership transition is to try it

Experiments with Your Network

> *In the next three days, talk to three people outside your business unit or company; learn what they do, how it helps the company, and how it may apply to your work.*

> *In the next three weeks, reconnect with people outside the company who may shed useful light on your work, industry, or career. Have lunch.*

> *Make a list of five senior people you need to get to know better. Figure out ways to strengthen your relationship over the next three months.*

and thus discover it for yourself. For a quick start on this step, see the sidebar "Getting Started: Experiments with Your Network."

You can start working now to connect differently. Develop relationships outside your group, sector, and even industry. Seek outside expertise. Work on understanding the office politics of moving into the senior ranks. Find ways to get to know people at least two levels above and, often, in a different unit or area—even when doing so feels instrumental. Get involved in, and contribute to, key initiatives that provide excuses to meet people above and below you. Work on raising your profile. Cultivate relationships outside your company, and use what you learn outside to connect to different people within your firm and to add value beyond operational delivery. Understand that what is important to those with control over your fate is probably different from what you might be delivering. Figure out your market value. Find kindred spirits. The sidebar "Practical Steps to Expand Your Network" offers a variety of ways you can cultivate new connections.

Practical Steps to Expand Your Network

- Spend time at a start-up within your business sector. Consider why incumbents rarely lead the way in new products and services.

- Attend a conference you have never before attended. Meet at least three new people. Follow up with them afterward.

- Start a LinkedIn or Facebook group. Be the connector for this group of people.

- Spend a day with a millennial in your company. Learn more about how she uses social media.

- Get in touch with a venture capitalist. Find out how he thinks about leadership and innovation.

- Teach a course at a university or local college. Learn from your students.

- Be a guest speaker at a local or national event. Use it to build or strengthen your brand around a particular area of expertise.

- Go to lunch with a peer from a competing company. Learn more about your market value.

- Start a blog. Find out who reads it.

- Take advantage of your next business trip to connect with someone you've lost track of. Have this person help you connect with someone new.

CHAPTER 3 SUMMARY

✓ As you embark on the transition to leadership, networking *outside* your organization, team, and close connections becomes a vital lifeline to who and what you might become.

✓ The only way to realize that networking is one of the most important requirements of a leadership role is to *act*.

✓ If you leave things to chance and natural chemistry, then your network will be narcissistic and lazy.

✓ You need operational, personal, and strategic networks to get things done, to develop personally and professionally, and to step up to leadership. Although most good managers have good operational networks, their personal networks are disconnected from their leadership work, and their strategic networks are nonexistent or underutilized.

✓ Network advantage is a function of your BCDs: the breadth of your contacts, the connectivity of your networks, and your network's dynamism.

✓ Enhance or rebuild your strategic network from the periphery of your current network outward as a first step toward increasing your outsight on your self:

– Seek outside expertise.

– Elicit input and perspectives of peers from different functional or support groups.

Be More Playful with Your Self

N MY TWENTY-FIVE YEARS OF teaching on leadership, I have found that one thing has remained unchanged: people's strong and unflinching desire to be true to themselves, and their equally strong aversion to doing things that make them feel like fakes. One of the most important motivators of any behavior is the belief that it is a fundamental expression of ourselves. That is exactly what gets us into trouble. Even when it comes to the most basic of leadership skills—listening, for example—people who are not very good at a skill will say that when push comes to shove, they don't practice more of the skill, because they don't feel genuine if they have to force themselves to do it.

Authenticity has become a topic of endless debate and fascination.[1] You can buy many books on how to be more authentic at work and can sign up for countless courses on how to be a more authentic leader.[2] Clearly, many of us are finding it problematic to just be ourselves.

One reason we're having trouble with authenticity is that we make more frequent and more do-it-yourself transitions today.[3] When we are working at improving our game, our authentic sense of self is a compass. It helps us navigate choices and work toward our goals. But when we are looking to change our game, authenticity is an anchor that easily keeps us from sailing forth.

FIGURE 4-1

Increasing your outsight by rediscovering your self

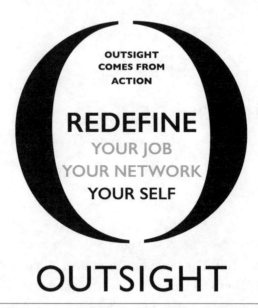

This chapter shows how authenticity is misunderstood and highly overrated when it comes to making the transition to new and unfamiliar roles. Because doing things that don't come naturally can make you feel like an impostor, authenticity easily becomes an excuse for staying in your comfort zone. The trick is to work toward a future version of your authentic self by doing just the opposite: stretching way outside the boundaries of who you are today (figure 4-1). This chapter shows you how.

Too Much Myself

When I first started teaching MBA students at Harvard, I was a dismal failure. I was young and had no business experience. Although I was a reasonable presenter, I hadn't yet learned the craft of leading a highly interactive yet structured discussion that ultimately concluded with a set of practical and concrete take-aways. My course ratings were at the bottom of the distribution; I was rapidly losing confidence in my ability to establish my authority in the classroom. I wasn't credible.

Many senior colleagues tried to help. Most offered well-meaning but relatively useless advice, all a version of this: "You have to be yourself in the classroom." The problem, however, was that I was being *too much* myself: too academic, too nervous, too dull, too distant. I invested a lot of time in watching skilled instructors conduct their classes, but everything they did was highly personal: their anecdotes, their life lessons, their jokes, even the ways they walked and talked to create a sense of theater. I wasn't sure what I could learn from them, and none of it seemed very serious—I wasn't sure I wanted to teach in the same style they did, either.

One day, a star professor came to watch me teach and offered some advice that I'll never forget. Now, you need to picture what our teaching amphitheaters look like—a huge, crescent-shaped room with ascending rows, and a pit, with the professor's desk at the bottom.

The less confident professors, like me, hunched near their desk at the bottom of the pit, close to their notes and far from the students. The experienced teachers marched up and down the aisles, taking up all the space and keeping all ninety of the students on their toes.

My colleague gave me very specific advice:

Your problem is that you think this is all about the content of what you are teaching. That has little to do with it. It ultimately comes down to power and turf. When you walk into this room, you should have one and only one mission: to make it crystal clear to every single one of your students that this is your room and not their room. And there's only one way you can do that, since they occupy the space all day long for the whole of the year. You have to be a dog and mark your territory in each of the four corners. Take every single inch of the space. Start with the top, where they think they are safe from your glance. See who is reading the Wall Street Journal, *who has underlined the case and who has left it blank, what kind of notes they have, and whether those notes have anything to do with the class. Get up close and personal when you talk to them, whisper in their ear, put your arm around them, pat them on their backs. Touch them. Show them that not even the person in the middle seat of the middle row is safe—squirm your way in. While you're at it, if they've got food and you're hungry, help yourself, take a bite. Then and only then will they know that it's your room and not their room. Once you've got that, you can think about the content that you want them to learn.*

I was horrified by this advice. I preferred my own ineffective approach by far—spending long nights over-preparing my cases and making sure I knew all the facts and figures so there would be no question I couldn't answer. But I was desperate enough by then to try it. One day I just started doing what he suggested.

The results were mixed at first. It felt uncomfortable, contrived, contrary to my values as a serious researcher. The students, by and large, didn't like my getting in their faces. But I began to get more of their attention, and after a while, my new way of behaving in the classroom started to feel like fun. It loosened me up, and I began to know my students better—I learned how they thought about the world and what they wanted to learn.

My objectives for the class shifted from delivering content to orchestrating an impactful learning experience. What I first dismissed as silly theatrics and emotional manipulation, I later came to value as a necessary approach to pedagogy that made the learning stick. I started to see different things in the antics of my more successful colleagues and became more willing to take risks. I stopped worrying about looking foolish. Of course, my learning accelerated. Over time, my ratings improved. I had acted my way into a new way of thinking.

Chameleons and True-to-Selfers

Where do we draw the fine line between authenticity and self-protection? I once studied a group of professionals who were stepping up from analytical and project work to advising clients and selling new business. The shift to client work was a classic do-it-yourself transition. In many cases, the investment bankers and consultants were expected to step up to the new role long before they earned a new title; in other cases, they were promoted without much change in formal job responsibilities, and the amount of client work they took on was left up to them (with major paycheck consequences, of course).

In the process, I stumbled upon an interesting contrast in how people making work transitions approach the problem of authenticity and some counterintuitive findings about the fastest path to an authentic yet different self. Most of the people I studied felt incompetent and insecure in this new capacity, and the advice they received was rarely helpful. They were frequently told to be more aggressive, to act with more confidence, or to develop their presence. As one investment banker told me, "At the end of my first year as a vice president, the feedback to me was, 'Your technical skills are great. Now, think more innovatively, seize the ball, and be more aggressive in your client meetings.' I think what they really wanted was for me to start thinking like a partner, to be the senior guy, not the adjunct to somebody else—to sort of try to be a bigger presence."

One group, which I called the *true-to-selfers*, tried to be themselves by focusing on what they knew how to do and felt

Barack Obama as a Chameleon

In his biography about Barack Obama before Obama became president, David Remnick calls him a "shape-shifter," because "Obama could change styles without relinquishing his genuineness."[a] Alec MacGillis, who reviewed Remnick's book, explains Obama's improbable rise in terms of this quality: "It is a path that required extreme agility—something more than the chameleon-like expedience that Obama's detractors saw in him."[b]

Another reviewer, Gary Willis, summarizes Remnick's explanation of Obama's fluidity: "Accused of not being black enough, he could show that he has more direct ties to Africa than most African Americans have. Suspected of not being American enough, he appealed to his mother's Midwest origins and accent. Touring conservative little towns in southern Illinois, he could speak the language of the Kansan grandparents who raised him. He is a bit of a chameleon or shape-shifter, but he does not come across as insincere—that is the importance of his famous 'cool.' He does not have the hot eagerness of the con man. Though his own back-

comfortable doing. The others, the *chameleons*, experimented with radically new and different ways of behaving and being, much as I did when I was trying to improve my teaching style.

The chameleons borrowed liberally from a diverse set of their more successful colleagues. They imitated their colleagues' demeanor—how they walked and talked, the jokes they made, their styles for establishing credibility. As one person put it, "You're trying on different personas as you might try on different suits." Often, they didn't get it right at first. Frequently, they felt foolish. The new behaviors felt unnatural, but the chameleons ground is out of the ordinary, he has the skill to submerge it in other people's narratives, even those that seem distant from his own."[c]

Obama worked hard to develop his broad stylistic repertory, says Remnick: "He subtly shifted accent and cadences depending on the audience: a more straight-up delivery for a luncheon of businesspeople in the Loop [in downtown Chicago]; a folksier approach at a downstate V.F.W. [a veterans organization]; echoes of the pastors of the black church when he was in one. Obama is multilingual, a shape-shifter . . . Like the child of immigrants who can speak one language at home, another at school, and another with his friends—and still be himself—Obama crafted his speech to fit the moment. It was a skill that had taken years to develop."[d]

a. David Remnick, *The Bridge: The Life and Rise of Barack Obama* (New York: Vintage Books, 2010).

b. Alec MacGillis, "Review: *The Bridge: The Life and Rise of Barack Obama*," *New Statesman*, May 12, 2010, www.newstatesman.com/books/2010/05/barack-obama-remnick-black.

c. Garry Wills, "Behind Obama's Cool," *New York Times*, April 7, 2010.

d. Remnick, *The Bridge*.

changed their suits anyway. They were trying to figure out who they might be in these dramatically different circumstances.

This kind of identity stretching comes more naturally to some people than others. Psychologist Mark Snyder identified the profile and psychology of chameleons (or "shape-shifters," as one of Barack Obama's biographers describes him) as people who are naturally able and willing to adapt to the demands of a situation without feeling like a fake.[4] Chameleons have core selves defined by their values and goals and have no qualms about shifting shapes in pursuit of their convictions (see the sidebar "Barack Obama as a Chameleon").

Are You a Chameleon or a True-to-Selfer (or a Hybrid)?

Here are some sample items from psychologist Mark Snyder's "self-monitoring" questionnaire:[a]

1. I find it hard to imitate the behavior of other people.

2. My behavior is usually an expression of my true inner feelings, attitudes, and beliefs.

3. At parties and social gatherings, I do not attempt to do or say things that others will like.

4. I can only argue for ideas I already believe.

5. I can make impromptu speeches even on topics about which I have almost no information.

6. I guess I put on a show to impress or entertain people.

7. When I am uncertain how to act in a social situation, I look to the behavior of others for cues.

"Yes" answers to items 5, 6, and 7 are associated with a chameleon profile, while "yes" answers to items 1–4 are typical of "true-to-selfers."

a. Mark Snyder, "Monitoring Scale," University of Washington, 1974, http://faculty.washington.edu/janegf/selfmonitoring.htm.

True-to-selfers, in contrast, view situational demands that push them away from their natural styles as threats to their authenticity. Their self-definitions are more all-encompassing, including not only their innermost values, but also their leadership styles, speech, dress, and demeanor. The sidebar "Are You a Chameleon or a True-to-Selfer (or a Hybrid)?" presents examples of Snyder's self-evaluation questions that can help you determine to what extent you are a chameleon.

Chameleons often advance more rapidly in the early years of their careers because they are relatively flexible and others are more likely to see them as leaders.[5] The sidebar "The Quintessential Chameleon" retells the famous story of Michael Lewis at Salomon Brothers. As I observed in my study, acting like a chameleon or a true-to-selfer produces different outcomes—in how others perceive you, how much help you get, and how fast you learn about work and about yourself.

Like Lewis's approach, the efforts of the chameleon professionals I was training got the attention of senior mentors, who saw that these professionals were trying to step up to the new role. The efforts made the seniors more apt to coach and mentor the new professionals, to share why and how they, the mentors, did what they did—one senior partner called this type of coaching "unveiling the mysteries." The senior executives shared their tacit knowledge about nuances that made all the difference—how to frame a meeting, how to build peer relationships with clients, how to diagnose the politics, how to notice the subtle positioning around controversial ideas, and so on.[6] They also shared something that is even more important: a point of view about what it takes to become a trusted adviser. Their endorsement and perspective also helped the chameleons to crystalize a sharper image of what and who they wanted to be like. Knowing how hard it can be to learn these kinds of things from someone who is very different stylistically, some mentors suggested more appropriate role models.

The chameleons also learned a great deal from their own emotional reactions as they experimented with alien behavior. Sometimes they confirmed what they always suspected about

The Quintessential Chameleon

In his best-selling book *Liar's Poker*, Michael Lewis describes how he rose from new, callow trainee fresh out of Princeton and the London School of Economics to become a highly successful bond salesman at Salomon Brothers, which was then one of Wall Street's premier investment firms. As he tells it, his chameleon personality proved to be a great strength in his career:

> Thinking, as yet, was a feat beyond my reach. I had no base, no grounding. My only hope was to watch the salesmen around me and gather what I advice I could.
>
> I had the ability to imitate. It enabled me to get inside the brain of another person. To learn how to make smart noises about money, I studied the two best Salomon salesmen I knew . . . My training amounted to absorbing and synthesizing their attitudes and skills.
>
> My job was a matter of learning to think and sound like a money spinner. Thinking and sounding like Alexander was the next best thing to being genuinely talented which I wasn't. So I listened to the master and repeated what I heard, as in kung fu. It reminded me of learning a foreign language. It all seemed strange at first. Then one day, you catch yourself thinking in the language. Suddenly words you never realized you knew are at your disposal. Finally you dream in the language.
>
> Each day Alexander called and explained something new. After several months of struggling, I began to catch on . . . I would call three or four investors and simply parrot what Alexander had just said. They would think me, if not a genius, then at least astute . . . Before long they wouldn't speak to anyone else but me.[a]

a. Michael M. Lewis, "From Geek to Man," in *Liar's Poker: Rising Through the Wreckage on Wall Street* (New York: W. W. Norton & Company, 1989).

themselves; other times they were surprised by what they learned. Their outsight stuck because it was grounded in their direct experiences instead of introspective speculation. One consultant told me, for example, that he realized that the "witty possible self" with which he had experimented was never going to be him: "I am not going to get up there and entertain the client with great wit. Is that a weakness? I need to develop some of those skills, but it's not going to be a mainstay of my repertoire. I'm confident in the person I've become and that my behavior will play reasonably well." Another chameleon told me how much he learned from deviating from his sense of self to a degree that "depressed" him: "I had a naive view of what it meant to be more forceful. I was not open to exploring what the client believed; nor did I show I cared about their response. I realized it was better to stick to my normal style, but to modify it slightly. My perception of myself is changing. It's scary and painful, but I'm learning a lot."

The true-to-selfers, by contrast, stuck to behaviors and styles that worked for them in the past. They sought to prove their competence by demonstrating technical mastery, citing their reliance on "substance rather than form." Often, they concluded that some of their successful seniors were "all talk and little content"—an unappealing aspiration for people whose professional identity was founded on their analytic wizardry. They believed that technical mastery was a more authentic strategy than that of their chameleon counterparts and was thus it a source of pride. But the clients wanted more than a great analysis or the "right answer"; they sought a personal connection and a point of view on their business. After a while, the true-to-selfers' seniors concluded that the true-to-selfers were just not getting it, and so the mentors invested less time in helping this group learn. Not surprisingly, the true-to-selfers' learning curve was slower.

While true-to-selfers often succeed with strong expertise and operational excellence in many jobs, they can hit a wall as they enter the transition to more senior leadership roles. In these roles, how leaders are perceived becomes as important as what they know, and success requires internalizing a whole new way of being. Ironically, the true-to-selfers' attempts to remain authentic undermined their ability to grow into the kind of leader they aspired to become. The chameleons who "faked it until they became it" arrived much more quickly at a true but different, more skillful self: they acted their way into a new but authentic identity.

The biggest problem with the true-to-self approach is that it defines authenticity according to the past and, by consequence, defines change as a loss. One consultant put it this way: "In terms of my development, I have a huge hurdle in transitioning from seeing myself as 'the one who knows all the facts' to being an adviser to the client. It's like my whole basis for existence is cut away if I can't rely on having read more than everyone else, having looked at all the analysis and understood all the points of view."

This quote illustrates what Columbia University psychologist Tory Higgins calls a "prevention" orientation, as opposed to a "promotion" orientation.[7] When you are in promotion mode, you pursue your aspirations and focus on what you might gain from your efforts. In prevention mode, you work to ward off potential threats to your current sense of self and pay attention to what you might lose. As we'll see in this chapter, stepping up to leadership requires a promotion focus, but many of the challenges of stepping up evoke prevention reflexes.

Despite the value they seemed to place on being authentic, many of the true-to-selfers in my study weren't fully being true to themselves; they were holding back out of fear of getting it wrong. One of the consultants I interviewed told me, "My style is creative, argumentative, and demanding. But with clients, I am more careful, and measured; I joke around less, and I'm less speculative." In the same way that I hung on to my facts and figures for fear of what might happen if I really engaged with my students, the hesitant face that this consultant was showing to her clients was no closer to her true self than the chameleons' impression-management efforts.

The Trouble with Authenticity

Let's look more closely at what authenticity means before we next consider how it becomes problematic when we're trying to step up to a bigger leadership role. The classic definition of authenticity is "being true to oneself." This seems simple enough, but it raises an all-important question about identity: which self? We are many selves. As William James put it, "A man has as many selves as the roles he takes on."[8] Roles are the different hats a person wears: the hats vary, but the person wearing them is the same; she is always *true*. But which self is true when you step into an unfamiliar role? Most of us are used to managing different hats. It gets more complicated when one hat is the old, well-worn favorite and the other is a different style and color from what we typically wear. As one of the consultants that I cited above put it, "Where on the continuum between my joke-cracking, beer-guzzling, speculative party-animal, argumentative, stubborn, do-things-my-own-way, at-the-extreme, anarchic self that I am with my colleagues at the firm and the rigid, careful, calculated persona I show to my clients is the right place to be?"

Another conundrum about being true to yourself concerns the age-old gap between who you are now and who you'd like to become. Which is your true self: yesterday's version, today's, or tomorrow's? In a career's worth of studies, Stanford psychologist Hazel Markus showed that people's identities are based just as much on the future possibilities they envision for themselves as they are on their formative past and present states. Possible selves are important aspects of who you are today because they guide and motivate your current behavior as you strive to become more like a desired or ideal self.[9]

A second, equally problematic definition of authenticity is "sincerity," or coherence between what you feel and what you say or do. Interestingly, the word *sincere* literally means "without wax," from the Latin roots *sine* (without) and *cera* (wax).[10] Columns or statues that were "without wax" were more authentic, and their beauty was based on substance, not just a veneer. Taken too far, this definition of authenticity is unproductive. Yes, we all want leaders who are human and can admit their weaknesses. But that does not mean that they should express each doubt or thought that comes into their head. The definition of authenticity as coherence is especially tricky when you assume a new role, with all the discomfort and uncertainty that comes with it. As a novice, you might try to play the role that you think is expected, but you won't get it right or feel authentic from the start. Similarly, when you start speaking a second language or are learning to cook, you follow what you know of the rules or recipe, but you don't deviate or improvise. It doesn't feel natural.

A third popular definition of authenticity is "being true to one's values and purpose."[11] When leaders pursue purposes that are aligned with their personal values, they experience themselves—and are experienced by others—as authentic.[12] This definition gives you more degrees of freedom; people who act with this definition in mind might feel no qualms about using dramatically different behavioral tactics and self-presentation strategies in different situations. They see themselves not as impostors but as adaptive and flexible people who are trying to achieve something important.[13]

Consider, for example, one of the most stable personality traits: introversion or extroversion. Extroverts are gregarious; they love human interaction. They get their energy from being with people. Introverts are quiet; they need time alone or they are easily depleted. But research shows that even consummate introverts are capable of acting like extroverts for the sake of achieving a goal they value highly.[14] That's why the shy Robert was capable of acting like a veteran networker in the service of his goal to become a line manager. The trouble comes when we don't know what our desired end state actually looks like. In transitions, we must, paradoxically, move away from our former selves before we become clear on who we want to become (we'll look at this in more detail in chapter 5). And as we have seen, our work values are often firmly anchored in the requirements of our former roles and past experiences. So we will inevitably feel inauthentic when taking the first steps, as my consultants and bankers did.

A fourth authenticity dilemma lies in our lack of full control over our identities. We are social beings.[15] Our identities depend not only on how we see ourselves but also on *how others see us* and what they expect to see before they consider us part of any category, like "leader." We don't have to be slaves to popular opinion, but the people around us must recognize, encourage, and endorse our leadership efforts if the efforts are to take hold. Without them, it's hard to sustain a view of ourselves as leaders, and without a collective consensus—that's what a reputation is—it's hard to get the next jobs, projects, and assignments that will help us continue to grow our leadership capacity. The problem here is that we don't look or walk or talk the part yet, precisely because we are in transition. So we have to find a way

TABLE 4-1

How various definitions of authenticity can present hurdles to leadership

Definition of authenticity	The problem the definition poses
Being true to oneself	We act and think differently when we play different roles; we don't know how to think and act when we take on a new role.
Behavior that expresses "who one is"; the *sincerity* and transparency of an act and its ability to come off as natural and effortless	We lose credibility if we disclose everything we think and feel, especially when we are unproven.
Acting with *integrity*; making moral, value-based choices concerning one's actions rather than accepting socially imposed values and actions	People don't necessarily know or share our values, and our current values are anchored in what we have done in the past.
Being true to a *prototype* of an established category, e.g., looking and talking like a leader	The people around us won't give us the benefit of the doubt if we don't look the type, but "fake it till you make it" makes us feel just like that: a fake.

to "fake it till we become it," as my Harvard Business School colleague Amy Cuddy puts it.[16]

Whichever of these four ways we define authenticity, chances are that it will get in our way as we step up to leadership (table 4-1). As we'll see below, the stepping-up process demands that we stretch way outside our identity comfort zone at the same time that it evokes strong identity self-protection reflexes: when we feel under threat because we are not sure if we will measure up, can perform, or be evaluated positively or even if all the effort is worth it, that's when we most want to stay true to our familiar selves.[17]

When Leading Makes You Feel Like a Fake

The situations in which we most stand to learn are also those that most challenge our sense of self. That's why stepping up to leadership makes so many of us feel as if we're faced with a choice between being a failure or a fake.

I have observed three common situations in which people are especially vulnerable to authenticity traps in stepping up to bigger leadership roles. First, as they take charge in a new role, some people have trouble managing a comfortable distance from their troops, either remaining too close or, alternatively, hiding behind titles and props to mask their discomfort. Second, others write off the need to sell their ideas and to inspire on a personal level as manipulation; they dismiss the hard and necessary work of building relationships with people they have little in common with as "using people," because they are afraid of their own power. Third, some people filter negative feedback through the lens of their authentic sense of self; they convince themselves that the more dysfunctional aspect of their "natural" leadership style is the crucial flip side of what makes them effective. And, in each of these situations, we are even more prone than usual to get caught in a bind between the behavioral norms of our national culture and our company's norms for leader behavior. These are exactly the sorts of situations in which increasing outsight on yourself becomes critically important. The sidebar "Leadership Challenges That Can Make You Feel Inauthentic" lists the situations that most often lead to these authenticity traps.

Leadership Challenges That Can Make You Feel Inauthentic

- Taking charge

- Selling your ideas (and yourself)

- Integrating negative feedback

Leading in a culture that is unfamiliar to you can exacerbate each of these challenges.

Too Close for Comfort

When Cynthia, a general manager in a health care organization, took charge in a new, much bigger job, she told her employees, "I want to do this job, but it's scary and I need your help."[18] In her previous role, heading up an ultrasound imaging business, she had felt very close to her smaller number of employees. A strong believer in collaborative leadership, she had been personally involved in most decisions, from product development to sales and advertising.

The transition upped the number of people reporting to her tenfold and multiplied the range of her businesses. "I was in shock that I was put into such a big role," she said. "I didn't feel ready so my reaction was to communicate 'I want to hear everything you have to say.'" She spent her first months scrambling to learn aspects of the business that were new to her, while trying to maintain her usual style as a hands-on, involved-with-people boss. With their boss loath to let go of her personal involvement in all the details, her direct reports were happy to let her shoulder the responsibility.

"I was so tired," she recalled, "I had always been entirely approachable. I thought it would work in a bigger job but I couldn't impact five thousand people directly, as I had before." Reflecting on her transition some years later, Cynthia concluded: "Being authentic doesn't mean that you can be held up to the light and people can see right through you. You don't need to spill your beans."

Particularly when it comes to taking charge in roles that are bigger in scale and scope, the personal touch and disclosure that can work so well on a smaller scale need to be replaced with a different way of leading. Delegating and communicating appropriately is only part of the problem. A deeper-seated issue is getting the balance of distance and closeness from the front lines right.[19] For Cynthia, the question of closeness versus distance presented an acute authenticity dilemma, one she eventually overcame: "I realized that as a leader you need some mystery and some unpredictability; you have to be very human at times, very "CEO-like" at others. People need to see you as one of them but they don't want their leader to be just one of them."

Stanford psychologist Deborah Gruenfeld describes this dilemma as finding the right balance between being authoritative and in command on the one hand and being approachable and human on the other.[20] When you aim to be authoritative, you privilege your knowledge, experience, and expertise over the team's same qualities, maintaining a measure of distance to take charge. When you aim to be approachable, you privilege your relationships with people and their input and perspective, and you lead from your empathy and warmth. Leadership transitions challenge you to find the right balance. Cynthia played it too approachable at first, and it drained her. Some people play it too close because they are deeply conflicted about exercising the power of their formal position, as Cynthia did. Others play it too distant, hiding their private insecurities behind carefully constructed formal personae.

Playing with Their Reptilian Brain

A lot of people wonder about the line between motivating people to get on board and manipulating them into something they don't want to do. When it feels like manipulation, it provokes an authenticity crisis.

A senior manager at a transportation company, Anne had experienced great operational success and had the numbers to prove it. She had doubled revenues and operating margins, given the company a new strategic direction, and undertaken a fundamental reorganization of the company's core processes and structures. Yet her boss didn't find her inspirational as a leader, and she knew she was not communicating effectively in her role on her parent company's board.

The board's chairman was a broad-brush, big-picture thinker who often balked at what he perceived as her excessive detail orientation. The stylistic mismatch between them was large, and his feedback to her was "step up, do the vision thing." Anne found herself reluctant to favor what she perceived as an inauthentic focus on form over substance: "I always wonder what people mean when they say, 'He's not much of a manager but he's a good leader.' Leader of what? You have to do things to be a leader. We are in danger today of being mesmerized by people who play with our reptilian brains. For me, that's manipulation. I can tell a poignant personal story too, but I refuse to play on people's emotions. If the string is too obvious, I can't make myself do it." A typical true-to-selfer, Anne saw "envisioning" behaviors as unnecessary or even self-promoting showmanship: the facts should speak for themselves. Spending time crafting an emotional message or slogan felt inauthentic; she just couldn't bring herself to do it. But, was she being authentic or simply staying inside her comfort zone?

Many aspiring leaders share this common reticence to influence and inspire using a full arsenal of rhetorical strategies and emotional tactics. In part, the hesitation is based on our self-conception as rational, factual businesspeople. But as shown in chapter 2, who we are—and not the facts and figures—is what truly persuades. Former Ogilvy & Mather CEO Charlotte Beers makes this point nicely in her recent book *I'd Rather Be in Charge*.[21] As an up-and-coming leader, she says, you need to understand that "you are not the work." In a speech based on the book, she put it this way: "You have to learn to step out in front of the work. It's you who interprets, analyses and delivers the work that matters. If you are not the work, what are you? You are the fuel, the energy, the system that delivers the work and gets it seen and recognized. It is your unique delivery system. It's made up of who you are, what you believe, what you feel, and what you think."[22]

When you scratch the surface of your discomfort, you find squeamishness about wielding power and influence. If Cynthia was having problems coming to grips with her vulnerability, Anne was having trouble coming to grips with her power. One of the biggest questions that managers and other professionals are faced with is, "How do I get people to do stuff?" This age-old question is the subject of many volumes devoted to the various tactics and tips for influencing other people.[23] People don't get better at it, mainly because they feel uncomfortable wielding power and influence. But in fact, the only thing that differentiates leading from just using power is that leading is using mutual and reciprocal influence—power—in the service of accomplishing a collective goal.[24]

If you, as a leader, understand that getting people to do "stuff" is all about the higher goal of achieving the organization's goals, then any worry you might have about being perceived as inauthentic or manipulative falls away. When you are working in the service of higher goals, then it's not about you or your ego or your own career anymore. It's about achieving the goal of a collective win.

If it's hard for some people to sell their ideas, then it's even harder for them to sell themselves to senior management. Although you can convince yourself that it's for the common good when you are selling your ideas, you can feel selfish when you try to get to know people to advance your career. But deep down, you know that if you don't do it, your good ideas and strong potential won't be noticed. Here's how one manager I interviewed described his reluctance to sell himself: "I personally believe in being professional, but I slowly realized that networking is more important in this organization than elsewhere. So I try to build a network based on professionalism and what I can deliver for the business, not who I know. Maybe that's not smart from a career point of view. But I can't go against my beliefs. I believe in building a professional network. So, I have been more limited in networking up."

Many books and workshops extol the virtues of self-promotion, and my aim is not to repeat their message here. If you're working to get out of some authenticity traps, it's not about learning the tactics. It's about changing your mind-set. We have the most trouble networking up when we're not sure that our individual career aims will add value to the company—that's when they seem the most selfish. As you increase outsight on your capacity—by actually spending more time getting to know senior leaders (using, for example, the two-degree principle outlined in chapter 3)—you are also more likely to see your own advancement as extending your impact.

Shattering Your Positive Illusions

Anyone who has ever done a 360-degree assessment is familiar with the infamous *self-observer gap*, or the discrepancy between how we see ourselves and how others see us. Closing the gap is even harder when we suffer from *positive illusions*, the robust tendency to see ourselves in the best light possible, which blinds us to how others see us.[25]

As we saw, Jacob, the food company production manager, was shocked when he received his 360-degree feedback report. The biggest surprise came from his direct reports, who rated him near the bottom of the scale on emotional intelligence, rewarding and feedback, team building, and empowering. One team member wrote that Jacob too often neglected the experience of his colleagues; another opined that it was hard for Jacob to accept criticism. A third remarked that after an angry outburst, Jacob could suddenly make a joke, as if nothing had happened, not realizing the destabilizing effect of his mood change. For someone who genuinely believed that he had tried to generate trust among his people, Jacob found his subordinates' belief that he lacked self-control hard to swallow.

After the initial shock subsided, Jacob acknowledged that this was not the first time he received such feedback: some of his colleagues and subordinates had made similar criticisms a few years back. "I thought that I'd changed my approach," he reflected, "but I haven't really changed so much since the last time." Deep inside, he rationalized the feedback as an example of a typical predicament that leaders face: "Sometimes you have to be tough in order to deliver results, and people don't like it. You have to accept that as part of the job description." Of course, he was missing the point.

All of us have positive illusions about ourselves and our impact on others. Psychologists have concluded that these illusions are mostly a good thing; they boost our confidence and protect us from depression. We tend to think that we know more than we do and that we are better than we are, as in the fictional Lake Wobegon, where "all the women are strong, all the men are good-looking, and all the children are above average."[26] A College Board survey of nearly a million high school seniors, for example, shows that this Wobegon effect sets in early: 70 percent claimed "above average" leadership skills; only 2 percent believed they were "below average."[27]

Positive illusions become especially problematic when we use the term *leadership style* as a euphemism for dysfunctional behavior like arrogance, bossiness, disdain, and lack of control over our temper. Most of us are not jerks all the time or with everybody. We give our best to certain team members and reserve ill treatment for others.[28] Our fatal flaws can go unchecked for a long time not only because we're delivering results and getting positive feedback from those we did not mistreat (usually our bosses), but also because the bad behavior happens infrequently.

As psychologist Roy Baumeister has shown, we fail to recognize that human nature is such that we remember best what troubled us most, what hurt us, what went wrong.[29] He calls this the "bad is stronger than good" effect, and it explains how and why we can make huge efforts to change and it all goes down the drain when we "misbehave" occasionally in a moment of high stress or pressure. People's observations about us are biased toward detecting problems. No one is systematically counting good and bad behaviors and taking the average—we retain what we don't like about others, and we label those people accordingly.

Positive illusions also get us into trouble when we assume that the problematic facets of our "natural styles" are inextricably bound up with our greatest strengths. Even when we recognize personal weakness, we often see it as a necessary flip side of a strength we consider essential to our success. This is a very common reaction to negative feedback, especially in 360-degree assessments in which we receive a wealth of often contradictory feedback from the different parties in our entourage. Like Jacob, many people rationalize the criticism by saying, "Yes, but I am as demanding of myself, and they learn so much!" (And, "That's the dilemma of being a leader.")

Just as we make biased inferences about other people, we maintain very biased inferences about ourselves. For Jacob, as for many of us, the bad goes with the good. Yes, he can be explosive. But from his point of view, it's all part of the package that has allowed him to deliver results year after year, and these results are reconfirmed all the time. A positive illusion about himself as results-driven lets him recast his fatal flaw as a necessary and acceptable downside of a successful approach that has been proven by experience (so far) and to which he is unflinchingly committed. He does not realize that he succeeds despite his behavior, not (as he believes) because of it.

A great example of this phenomenon is Margaret Thatcher, whose visionary leadership was discussed previously. Those who worked with her knew she could be merciless if someone failed to prepare a case as thoroughly as she did, that she was capable of humiliating a staff member in public, that she was a bad listener, and that she believed compromise was cowardice. As she became known to the world as the "Iron Lady," Thatcher became more and more convinced of the rightness of her ideas and the necessity of her coercive methods to get the job done. She could beat anyone into submission with the power of her rhetoric and conviction, and she only got better at it. Eventually, she was ousted by her own cabinet.

I've often tried to imagine how Thatcher saw herself and how she might respond to 360-degree feedback on her leadership style. One of her throwaway lines in a famous BBC interview gives me a good idea: "When I'm out of politics," she said, "I'm going to run a business, it'll be called 'rent-a-spine.'" Having made her name on her steely and single-minded toughness, she came to believe it was the only way to get things done. Just like Jacob, she told herself, "Without my tenacity, where would we be?" even as ally after ally defected from her cause.

Constructive criticism ideally helps us revise our self-conceptions, but, sadly, most negative feedback will block learning by creating a defensive response (see, for example, the sidebar "Self-Assessment: What Are Your Authenticity Traps?").[30] As MIT professor Ed Schein notes, we just ignore the information, dismiss it as irrelevant, blame the undesired outcome on others or the nature of the job, or, most commonly, simply deny its validity—unless we get it from someone who we believe has our best interest at heart.[31] That's why it's so important to maintain a network that can give us just the kind of feedback we don't want to hear—something that Thatcher sorely lacked.

The Loudest Duck

Paris-based cosmetics firm L'Oréal is a very international workplace, so the company spends lots of effort sensitizing employees to the different behavioral norms that their coworkers bring from their countries of origin. At the same time, L'Oréal has a very distinct corporate culture. It values debate and believes that the best ideas emerge from creative conflict. This is a tall order for people who come from places like China, where they were taught from childhood that "the loudest duck gets shot." It's hard for people with this cultural background to be seen as leaders when they are working with people who learned instead that the squeaky wheel gets the grease.[32]

Finding authentic ways of being effective is even harder when you work in a multinational environment. What demonstrates that a person is in command, how one sells ideas, and even how one conveys feedback can be very culturally specific. For example, as my INSEAD colleague Erin Meyer finds, the ways you seek to persuade others and the kinds of arguments that you find persuasive are far from universal; they are deeply rooted in your culture's philosophical, religious and educational assumptions.[33] But, the common "template" for expressing one's authentic leadership—telling a very personal story about hardship one has overcome—is deeply American, culturally. For leaders from many other countries, this is not only an unnatural act but also an example of an American tendency to over-disclose and fail to keep an appropriate distance in business relationships. The sidebar "Culture and Confrontation at L'Oréal" shows some of the reactions people from different cultures had when asked to engage in confrontation.

Organizational culture is a double-edged sword. When it's strong, it's the glue that binds people together into a recognizable *we*. But strong cultures also have implicit prescriptions about what leaders are supposed to look and sound like, and those prescriptions are rarely as diverse as the talent pool of aspiring leaders. L'Oréal employees from cultures where direct confrontation is anathema understand that they are expected to challenge others ideas vigorously and why this behavior is prized. But it doesn't feel authentic to them.

Culture and Confrontation at L'Oréal

The following quotations illustrate the range of reactions that people of different cultures had when they were expected to take part in, and lead, debates at L'Oréal.[a]

- "L'Oréal culture, as everybody knows, is about allowing debate, being part of the process of debating a business idea, because if an idea cannot survive through this debating process, it is not a good idea, it is not something that can easily survive in the market. But confrontation to a Chinese is extremely negative. He's in a way saying no, and making the other party lose his face. So it's something that we try to avoid." (Chinese manager)

- "In a Japanese cultural context, confrontation is something that is rude, that is too aggressive, and that is just very impolite and disrespectful. There's a sales meeting, or a meeting with a lot of Japanese sales managers who don't speak English, plus the French management, plus the marketing team, where the French management would have a translator asking each Japanese sales rep, 'So what do you think about this?' 'What do you think about this?' 'Why do you think this?' . . . At first they were just shocked that they would be put on the spot in a meeting, with a lot of people. That is just an insult." (Japanese manager)

- "I think that in Italy, we try to avoid confrontation. We do express our disagreements, but in a very delicate—in a more diplomatic way compared to other countries. After a confrontation, when people told me, 'Please don't take it personal / ne le prends pas perso,' I just felt aggressed, and I do, I can't help it, I do take it personal." (Italian manager)

a. *Source:* From "L'Oréal Culture in a Multi-Cultural World: Confront or Avoid Confrontation?" training video, L'Oréal, February 2012.

Although many of us have become sensitive to cultural differences thanks to international assignments and the global teams in which we work, we still expect leaders to take the lead: to advance their ideas assertively, to claim credit for their ideas, to argue a clear point of view, and to do so with presence.[34] In one global company of Anglo-Dutch origin, high-potential individuals who did not hail from those cultures told me that success required impeccable English and a facility with word play—skills that they lacked and that placed them at a huge disadvantage. The kinds of presentations that made these managers visible to top management (as recommended in chapter 2) were moments of considerable stress for them.

You don't even need international diversity to get competing norms for how to behave. Across the globe, men and women are taught very different standards for how to conduct themselves; male standards invariably come closer to what most people code as leadership. So in the workplace, women face the infamous double-bind, whereby if they "act like a leader," they are too manly and aggressive, but if they "act like a woman," their leadership can go unrecognized, especially as they position themselves to move up to the highest levels.[35] Asian women in particular struggle with this catch-22 and are often seen as both too aggressive and not assertive enough, depending on the context. Here's what one of them told me: "In Asia, I was told I was too bossy. In Europe, they tell me I am not bossy enough, that I need to have more leadership, stand up and present my ideas, have a stronger voice . . . My personal feeling is that to be seen as high potential, you have to be almost a man, so what is the point of being a woman? The senior women I know are not different from men. It is a challenge. I do not fit the prototype; I cannot change my personality to fit this. My personal leadership style is not authoritarian. How can I be more authoritative and look and behave like a senior leader?"

Research shows that your drive to improve and advance grows hand in hand with recognition from people who are valued by your organization and whose opinion you yourself value.[36] When the identity you develop in one .cultural context manifests itself differently in a company or another group context, you might be shortchanged of leadership recognition, one of the key components of leader identity development. Without recognition and endorsement, you become even quieter. Soon your motivation to lead is diminished.

The answer to this ubiquitous authenticity dilemma isn't obvious, because going native is rarely the answer. Striking the right balance, as we'll see below, often depends on finding role models who are both successful and similar to you either in terms of culture or in terms of stylistic preferences.

Stretch Beyond Your Current Self-Concept

LinkedIn's Reid Hoffman and coauthor Ben Casnocha famously said that a lot of people feel about networking the same way they feel about flossing: it's good for you, but no fun to do.[37] I've found the same when it comes to working on yourself. Too often it feels like a lot of work. In fact, researchers in my field, organizational behavior, use the term *identity work* to describe all the things we do to form, repair, maintain, or revise our unitary sense of who we are.[38] This is the stuff of the self-help section of your favorite bookstore. It's not fun, and neither does it work when you're in transition to something new.[39]

What's the alternative? Becoming more playful with your own identity. Doing *identity play* instead of *identity work*.[40]

What do I mean by playing around with your identity? Let me explain first what research says about the difference between work and play. It's actually not about the activity itself—you can

Self-Assessment:
What Are Your Authenticity Traps?

Consider an area in which you have received negative or constructive feedback more than once or from more than one person, and on which you'd like to make progress. You might have been encouraged, for example, to delegate more, or to adapt your leadership style, or to offer your point of view instead of an analysis of the facts and data. Below, write down what the suggestion was:

_____

Now, consider what might be holding you back from making progress in this area. Which, if any, of the following statements do you agree with?

	YES	NO
1. I believe a good leader is someone who stays close to the troops.	_____	_____

play at work and work at play—it's about the mind-set with which you approach any activity.[41]

When you are working, you're serious. You set goals and objectives, are mindful of your time, and try to get progressive improvements. You're not going to deviate from the straight and narrow. When you're playing, you're, well, playful. You lose track of time. You meander. There's no real utility to what you are doing; you don't have to follow the rules. You enjoy yourself, are curious, and discover new things.[42] The great benefit of a playful approach to anything is that it increases your creativity.[43]

	YES	NO
2. The best way to influence people is to stick to the facts. Playing on people's emotions is manipulation.	_____	_____
3. It's one thing to network to get buy-in for a business goal, but I won't network to advance my career.	_____	_____
4. I was taught not to attract too much attention to myself or to my ideas. So I tend to be quieter in meetings than most people around me.	_____	_____
5. My problematic behaviors have a positive side that I value (e.g., I have low emotional intelligence, but that helps me deliver on the task).	_____	_____

Each "yes" response suggests a significant vulnerability to one of the authenticity traps discussed in this chapter.

The same goes when you are playing with who you might become. You explore possibilities without committing to any of them. You're in essence flirting with your future possible selves rather than constantly evaluating today's version of yourself against a nonexistent ideal, testing it for a "committed relationship," or trying to get approval from others in light of a limited and not-yet-personalized view of their requirements.[44] So, you're more open to what you might learn about yourself.

In three important ways that I will discuss, identity play frees you from the authenticity traps described earlier. First, when you are playing around with your self-identity, it's OK to borrow liberally from different sources. Second, playfulness changes your mind-set from a performance focus to a learning orientation. You're no longer trying to protect and defend your old identity from the threat that change brings. You're just exploring. Third, your goal is actually to be inconsistent from one day to the next, to iterate—and even to revise—your own story. You're not being a fake; you're just experimenting with diverse possibilities before settling on a new direction. Below are a few guidelines for how to do it.

Steal Like an Artist

If there is one occupation that prizes authenticity, it's art. At the same time, no one besides an artist knows better that nothing is original.

Artist and writer Austin Kleon talks about the feedback he got when he first started doing his signature newspaper-blackout poetry. He creates these works by circling newspaper words and phrases that interest him and blacking out the rest with a marker. When told about someone who had been doing similar work for some time, Kleon looked that artist up and ultimately uncovered a sequential line of artists who took their inspiration from one another over the years.

Through this "genealogical" research that took him back to the 1700s and various "genealogical branches," Kleon realized that the end product, his own work, was the unique result of many and varied influences. As he reflected on his creative process, he distilled a few basic principles, which he parlayed into a *New York Times* best seller, *Steal Like an Artist.*[45] Here are a few of his insights:

- Nothing is original.

- You're only going to be as good as the stuff (or the people) you surround yourself with.

- Don't wait until you know who you are to get started.

- Copy your heroes.

Too many people get hung up worrying that they are an impostor or a phony, Kleon says: "If I'd waited to know who I was or what I was about before I started 'being creative,' well, I'd still be sitting around trying to figure myself out instead of making things. In my experience, it's in the act of making things and doing our work that we figure out who we are" (see figure 4-2).

But there is a trick here, too. There is a big difference between imitating someone wholesale and imitating aspects of what the person does, borrowing the best bits and pieces from different people to compose your own unique collage, which you then modify and improve. Some of my investment bankers and consultants did this naturally, consciously borrowing different styles and tactics from their more successful seniors. My executives

FIGURE 4-2

Austin Kleon's distinction between good and bad theft

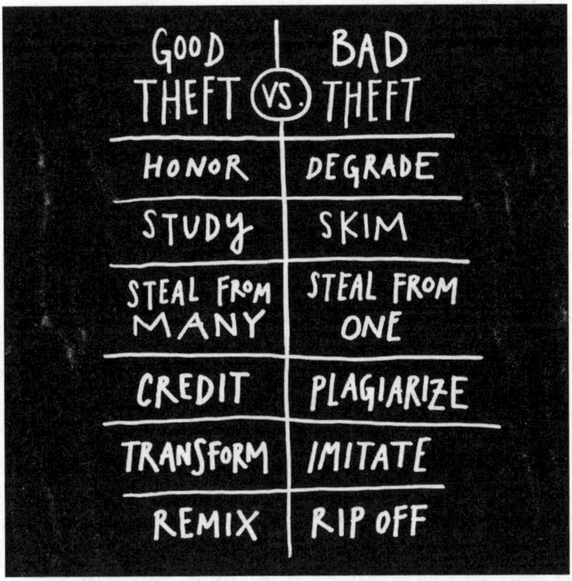
GOOD THEFT
VS.
BAD THEFT
HONOR
DEGRADE
STUDY
SKIM
STEAL FROM MANY
STEAL FROM ONE
CREDIT
PLAGIARIZE
TRANSFORM
IMITATE
REMIX
RIP OFF

Source: Excerpted from *Steal Like an Artist*, copyright 2012 by Austin Kleon. Used by permission of Workman Publishing Co. Inc. All rights reserved.

who believed they had to find the perfect role model, in turn, had a harder time and felt more inauthentic when they tried to imitate supposed perfection. As the writer Wilson Mizner says, if you copy from one author, it's plagiarism, but if you copy from many, it's research.[46] That's what Cynthia did, and today she advises people to identify leaders who do well what they are trying to learn and watch them carefully. For Kleon, what's really important is not to just steal someone's style, but also to *steal the thinking behind the style* so that you can somehow get a glimpse into that person's mind and internalize her way of looking at the world.

Aim to Learn

Let's admit it: one of the biggest reasons we don't stretch beyond our current selves is that we are afraid to fail, to suffer a hit to our performance. As Harvard psychologist Robert Kegan and his co-authors find, most people at work "divert considerable energy every day to a second job that no one has hired them to do: preserving their reputations, putting their best selves forward, and hiding their inadequacies from others and themselves."[47]

Of course, all of us want to perform well in a new situation, to get the right strategy in place, to be rewarded for our performance, and perhaps to get to a new place in our careers. But goals that are too narrowly focused on our performance can diminish how much we're willing to risk in the service of learning. When we are stepping up to new roles, performance goals can actually backfire, because the less we learn, the lower our chances of success.

Consider what happed to Thomas, the head of a large Mexican sales team that accounts for 40 percent of his country's revenues. Thomas was being groomed for a top sales job. To expose him to other parts of the business, his boss appointed him to the management board for Mexico, a role Thomas described as both his biggest developmental opportunity and his biggest challenge: "Now I have to be able to talk about all the product groups, including those I have not been involved in at all, and all the functions, including R&D, finance, and marketing. Basically, I have to learn 40 percent of the business." Knowing he was expected to make an impact, he tried to make up for his inexperience with a bigger stage presence, faking confidence instead of showing vulnerability.

A turning point came when Thomas was asked to give the board a progress report on a project outside his area of expertise. Knowing that he would encounter resistance to his proposal, Thomas understandably worried about someone's hijacking the discussions while he gave the presentation. To keep things from getting out of control, he just kept marching through his slides, sticking to the script despite the mounting frustration of his audience. He never gave the board members a chance to engage in a frank discussion of the issues. In search of recognition and approval, he lost sight of a larger purpose and focused instead on protecting his public image as an expert. So he missed a chance to learn what they thought. Naturally, his recommendations were not adopted, and it took him months to learn why.

In a series of ingenious experiments, psychologist Carol Dweck has shown how concerns about how we will appear to others inhibit learning on new or unfamiliar tasks.[48] When people are driven by what she calls "performance goals," they are motivated to show others that they have a valued attribute (e.g., intelligence, humility, good values) and they are looking to validate for themselves a self-image as someone who has this attribute. When people are driven by "learning goals," by contrast, they are motivated to develop a valued attribute.

Performance- or image-focused people prefer tasks that will help them look good, as opposed to tasks that will help them learn, and are more likely to approach highly visible leadership situations as just that: performances. So, according to Dweck's studies, these people experience more anxiety and apprehension, are less likely to work on their weaknesses, tend to talk more and listen less, and are more likely to stick with the familiar but inappropriate approach, much as Thomas did.

A good counterexample of Thomas's performance focus is what Chris Johnson (from chapter 3) did in his first meeting with the country managers who felt that his enterprise software implementation was being shoved down their throats. Johnson knew they weren't happy, and he expected a lot of pushback. So, he threw out the prepared talk and just spent an entire morning doing Q&A instead. This approach took a lot of guts. The morning was brutal. The managers just went at him. But Johnson wanted to learn about their frame of mind. So, as he tells it, he played it like Muhammad Ali taking the punches from George Foreman. After lunch, Johnson took a different, more playful but also tougher tack. "How many of you would like my job?" he asked. When no hands went up, he told them, "If [it] doesn't work, I get fired. If I get fired, [my boss] is going to pick one of you to run it. So here is the deal: if you don't want my job, you'd better make this work."

Managers and other professionals are constantly plunged into situations that elicit performance goals. For example, they might have to take charge in a new role, make board presentations or other highly visible expositions, or respond to negative formal performance feedback. When you are in performance mode, the game is about presenting yourself in the most favorable light: minimizing risks and maintaining positive illusions. A learning mode leads to a more playful approach, one that allows you to reconcile your natural yearning for authenticity in how you work and lead with an equally powerful motivator: growing and, most of all, learning about and extending possibilities for yourself.

Don't Stick to Your Story

Writer Salman Rushdie once wrote: "Those who do not have power over the story that dominates their lives, power to retell it, rethink it, deconstruct it, joke about it, and change it as times change, truly are powerless because they cannot think new thoughts."[49] As we have seen, leaders use their stories to personally inspire people. A tried-and-true way of finding the right personal story to convey one's values or purpose is to reflect on defining moments in our lives, when our mettle was tested in some important way, when a life event taught us an important lesson.[50] But just as our working identities can get outdated, so can our stories. As cognitive scientist Dan Dennett puts it "Our tales are spun, but for the most part, we don't spin them; they spin us."[51] We need to feel OK about revising the stories every once in a while, when they no longer meet our purposes.

Former Ogilvy & Mather CEO Charlotte Beers gives a great example about a leader she coached. Maria held an image of herself as a "mother hen with her chicks all around."[52] The image came from a story about a time when Maria had to sacrifice herself to take care of her extended and matriarchal family. But as Beers pointed out to her, the story and the image she carried around from it were keeping her from stepping up to a big leadership role. The story fit her image of a friendly and loyal team player and peacekeeper—not a leader who got the big assignment she wanted. Together, Beers and Maria looked for another defining moment, a time when as a young woman Maria had left her family to travel the world for eighteen months. This story was more in keeping with the courage Maria felt it took to lead her creative group. Acting from her sense of self in that story, she got the promotion.

Dan McAdams, who has spent his whole career studying life stories, says that a person's identity is "the internalized and evolving story that results from [the person's] selective appropriation of past, present and future."[53] McAdams's statement isn't just academic jargon. He is saying that you have to believe your own story, to internalize it, but it is changing all the time, according to what you need it to do. As your purposes change, so should you change your stories, so that your narrative best accounts for your new aspirations and resonates with the audience you are trying to win over. You are not inventing fiction, but selectively appropriating things that have made you who you are. That's why revising—or playing with—your story is a big part of stepping up.[54]

Be Like Water

"Be like water," says Hetain Patel, quoting Bruce Lee in one of my favorite TED talks, titled "Who Am I? Think Again."[55] Patel, a performance artist, is interested in identity precisely because we are many different selves. The son of Indian immigrants to Britain, he was always up against the limited, one-dimensional image that people would form of him in light of his appearance. In his playful yet serious discussion of authenticity, Patel talks about how he learned about himself by imitating his heroes: his father, Spider-Man, Bruce Lee, and his Chinese teacher (who happened to be a woman, so he got the intonation all wrong). For example, in one multimedia project, he grew a mustache to look like his father and recorded the results.

Bruce Lee, the great martial artist, fascinated Patel because Lee was constantly experimenting with new methods and inventing his own mix to improve his art. Lee believed that you should "use only that which works and take it from any place you can find it."[56] His mantra was "be like water:"[57] Don't get set into one form, adapt to different situations (as water flows), and grow from them.

Likewise, Patel concludes: "Contrary to what we might usually assume, imitating something can reveal something unique.

So every time I fail to become more like my father, I become more like myself. Every time I fail to become more like Bruce Lee, I become more authentically me." Kleon basically says the same thing: "A wonderful flaw about human beings is that we're incapable of making perfect copies. Our failure to copy our heroes is where we discover where our own thing lives. That is how we evolve."[58] See the sidebar "Getting Started: Experiments with Your Self" for ideas on how to redefine your self-concept as you learn from new experiences and observing others.

GETTING STARTED

Experiments with Your Self

❭ *In the next three days, start finding heroes: people whose leadership you admire. Watch them closely.*

❭ *Over the next three weeks, get to know some of these heroes better. Find out who influenced them and how they think about what they do. Talk to them about their purpose in work and how they discovered it. Start your own collage, that is, try to incorporate useful qualities from these heroes into your own persona.*

❭ *In the next three months, find a context or situation that makes you uncomfortable. This could be giving a presentation, speaking at an industry forum, or even speaking out at important meetings. Set learning goals. Act as radically different from your normal behavior as you can.*

Learning, by definition, always starts with unnatural and often superficial behaviors that can make a person feel like a fake—a strategic, calculating, and utilitarian being instead of the genuine, spontaneous person we'd prefer to be. Finding an appropriate level of disclosure and friendliness with direct reports and learning to sell our ideas, manage our bosses, operate effectively in an alien culture, and tame our dark side doesn't always come naturally. Rather than adapting to new information and experiences, we tend to keep ourselves in a rigid box in the guise of authenticity. But sometimes, as Patel and Lee discovered, we're much better off being like water and letting new experiences and situations decide what shape our emerging true selves will take.

CHAPTER 4 SUMMARY

✓ Many of the typical challenges of stepping up to leadership make people feel like fakes: taking charge in a new role, selling their ideas, managing their higher-ups, working in an alien culture, and learning from negative feedback.

✓ Chameleons are comfortable shifting shapes and styles to fit each new situation; true-to-selfers, on the other hand, tend to feel inauthentic when asked to stretch outside their comfort zone.

✓ Authenticity traps really get you into trouble when you are stepping up to leadership, because what feels like the authentic *you* is the old self that you are trying to shed.

✓ One way to escape the authenticity trap is to think about experimenting with new behaviors as playing around with your sense of who you are instead of working on it. The new behaviors might feel unnatural in the beginning, but they help you figure out who you might want to be, without your actually committing to become it—playing gives you out-sight on yourself.

✓ Identity—who you are—is not just about the past; it's also the possibilities you envision for yourself in the future.

✓ Here are three ways you can play around with your sense of who you are:

- *Steal like an artist:* Observe a broad range of role models to create your own collage of things you want to learn from these models, and keep refining your style until it is effective and authentic.

- *Aim to learn:* Set learning goals, not just performance goals.

- *Don't stick to your story:* Try different versions, narrate different defining moments, and keep editing, much as you would your curriculum vitae.

Manage the Stepping-Up Process

So, YOU'VE BEEN WORKING on increasing your outsight by following some of the suggestions in the last three chapters. What happens next? How do these efforts add up to increase your leadership capacity? To answer these questions, you have to take a closer look at how change unfolds and at some of the common misconceptions about how it happens.

People often hope that they'll have some sort of conversion experience: a moment when it all snaps into place, after which nothing is the same again. This image comes from the archetypal stories we heard when we were growing up: the biblical story of Saul on the road to Damascus, for example. Struck down from his horse by the hand of God, he instantaneously became Paul and devoted his life to Christ thereafter. Conversion stories exist in every culture and religion. They tell about the one event that changed everything. But it's just not the way it really works.

A much better metaphor is the story of Ulysses, on his long, wandering journey back to Ithaca—a journey with many temptations to stray. We'll get lost along the way, lost enough to find ourselves, as Robert Frost put it.[1]

So it is with stepping up to play a bigger leadership role. It's not an event; it's a process that takes time before it pays off.

Our new actions are important, even if they sometimes seem superficial, because they provide some necessary quick wins and fresh information about what is possible. But there is rarely a straight line to the finish. Things get complicated. We get busy. Time pressure piles on. We almost always backslide or fail to stick to our commitments. Because we're rarely very good at our new roles at first, we are loath to let go of old behaviors. What slowly starts to become more and more apparent is that our goals for ourselves are changing. That's when reflecting on what we have been learning by doing becomes invaluable, so that the bigger changes that ensue are driven by a new clarity of self.

The Conversion of a Process Engineer

George, a manufacturing engineer, was part of a group of functional specialists, production supervisors, and engineers selected by their company to participate in a major reengineering project.[2] Somewhat bored after fifteen years in the company's operations group, George looked forward to this two-year assignment. He was eager to learn something new, to get out of the box. When he signed up, he had no idea what consequences the move would have for his career.

Working on the reengineering project profoundly changed how he thought about his organization and the purpose of his work. George acquired a big-picture view of his company and understood, for the first time, the extent to which his prior functional perspective was limited and parochial. Over time, he came to see himself as a systems thinker. He experienced a shift in how he saw his contribution, from doing great functional work to changing the organization to better serve the customer.

As these new ways of thinking took root, George found himself disconnecting more and more from his home-base work unit, where he no longer felt he really belonged, and instead seeking out opportunities to interact not just with other project team members but with a larger external community made up of others who had also been bitten by the process-engineering bug.

These new experiences and relationships led him to redefine his sense of self, his purpose in work, and his career ambitions. After the project ended, he had no desire to return to his old group. Working to change his organization was meaningful. It gave him a sense of making a difference, and he wanted to do more of it.

This change did not happen overnight but inched up on him as he worked on the project and became an ever-more-active participant in an industrywide community of process reengineers. At the start of the training that all the project members underwent, George learned the tools of business process redesign and came to understand notions like root-cause analysis and flow-charting. It was all quite abstract and theoretical, far removed from the real problems the team was being asked to solve. He was often as confused about what he was supposed to be doing as he was stimulated. To make sense of it all, George looked outside, attending conferences, hanging around with peers doing the same thing in other organizations, and reaching out to the gurus in this field. Over time, he started to understand enough about what they thought about complex systems to start coming up with his own ideas for his organization. His active participation in the world of reengineering made his new and often puzzling experiences come alive, replete with personal implications for a possible new identity as an agent for change.

Many of the leaders whose stories I have told in the preceding chapters started learning about leadership in an equally abstract way. They were exposed to classic leadership concepts, read the best sellers, hired coaches to help them improve their style, and thought hard about what they wanted and needed to change. But all that is a far cry from actually learning to do the work of leadership and coming to a deep-seated understanding of why leadership is important and personally meaningful. For that to happen, they had to live through a transition process, like George's, that was often more challenging than they first expected.

Process, Not Outcome

Most methods for changing ask you to begin with the end in mind, the desired outcome.[3] But in reality, knowing what kind of leader you want to become comes last, not first, in the stepping-up process.

George could have told you that he no longer felt challenged in his old job and that it lacked meaning for him. But no matter how much time he spent reflecting on where he wanted to go and who he wanted to become, he was never going to find the purpose he found in the reengineering work. Only his direct experiences led him to a deeper understanding of his desire for change and allowed him to construct a more attractive, concrete alternative.

Getting there wasn't easy. During the first year of the reengineering project, George had a hard time reconciling his new role as a change agent with his earlier views about what kind of work was worth doing. For example, he learned that he actually loved managing a team—something that had been a tedious chore for him before—when the work was something he cared passionately about. But there was a price to pay for the learning: as his thinking about his organization and its problems changed, he didn't fit in so well anymore with his old crowd.

So it is with the executives who attend my courses. After an intensive week learning about the ideas presented in the last three chapters, they go home with a personalized action plan. This plan is just meant to get them started; it is by no means a one-shot deal. More often than not, they initially commit to the low-hanging fruit, the obvious and immediate things they need to do to improve their key working relationships, extend their networks, and explore new projects. They add before they subtract, meaning that they focus mostly on what else they can do, before they start dropping things from their usual operating routines. In general, the executives tend to become very busy soon after they return to work. They get sidetracked and become frustrated with the slow pace of progress. Some of them start to give up. Those who stick to it, with help from each other via virtual group meetings and a second on-campus session, gradually start to see some evolution, but not without some hard thinking about what they must leave behind and what they will keep doing.

George and all my participants went through what I call the *stepping-up process*. This process is what happens in between A (where you are today) and B (where you eventually might arrive) (figure 5-1). Stepping up is a transition, and transitions are unpredictable, messy, nonlinear, and emotionally charged, for many reasons:[4]

- B is unknown and uncertain.

- A is no longer viable.

- There are many possible routes to B.

- B changes as we approach it.

The net result is that managing a transition is completely unlike shooting for a known outcome.[5] Think about it as the difference between making a dish following a recipe and becoming a great chef. When you are trying to make something that tastes good, you pretty much achieve the desired outcome if you get the right ingredients and follow the recipe. It's an input-output model, where the output can vary, from more to less tasty or

FIGURE 5-1

Stepping up to leadership is a process of moving from A to B[a]

Any process of personal change is composed of three parts: A, B, and the transition between them. A, our current state, is how we do things and who we are today. It may not be optimal, but it is familiar and comfortable because we know what to expect. We've been successful at A, and we know how we will be measured and evaluated when doing A. B, the future state we aspire to, is the unknown. It's where we think we are trying to go, but that's not always clear or well defined at the start, and it usually shifts while we are trudging through the transition. B tends to change as we change.

a. William Bridges, *Managing Transitions: Making the Most of Change* (Philadelphia: Da Capo Lifelong Books, 2009).

from looking more to less like the picture in the recipe book. With practice, most people can expect to become a better cook than they were at the start.

When you are trying to become a great chef, the inputs also matter, but there is no direct relationship between the time and effort you put in and the outcome you get. Becoming a great chef depends on conditions that increase the likelihood that your cooking will be inventive—conditions like training under a great chef, traveling to far-off places to learn about new ingredients, a serendipitous encounter with a famous food critic, and a strong network of the best food suppliers. But none of these will guarantee that you'll meet your goal. Success in this case depends on your becoming a different person from who you were at the start.

Stepping up to leadership is more like becoming a great chef than following a recipe. The process changes who you are in ways that you might not anticipate.

Stages of Stepping Up to a Bigger Leadership Role

Stage 1: Disconfirmation

- Feeling the gap between where you are and where you want to be

- Increased urgency to spur first action steps

Stage 2: Simple Addition

- Adding new roles and behaviors (without subtracting old ones)

- Increased outsight; getting quick wins on low-hanging fruit

Stage 3: Complication

- Back-sliding, setbacks

- Exhaustion from making time for both old and new behaviors; obstruction as the people around you encourage your "old" self

Stage 4: Course Correction

- Frustrations that raise bigger career questions

- Time to "bring the outsight back in": reflection on new experiences to reexamine old goals and make new ones

Stage 5: Internalization

- Changes that stick because they are motivated by your new identity and express who you have become

A Predictable Process

Although you can't anticipate what B will actually look like as you start stepping up to a bigger leadership role, you can anticipate predictable stages in the transition. In my research and teaching, I have observed that the process typically follows a sequence of five stages. You don't move from today's problematic state (stage 1) to competent leadership (stage 5) in one fell swoop but rather navigate a series of steps in between (see the sidebar "Stages of Stepping Up to a Bigger Leadership Role").

Disconfirmation

The stepping-up process almost always starts with a gap between where you are and where you want to be. That's the spark that motivates us to take action.

Indeed, most forms of adult learning and change start with some sort of dissatisfaction or frustration generated by information or feedback that disconfirms our expectations.[6] For years, psychologists using the carrot-and-stick analogy have stressed the importance of the stick, or a painful motivator, in sparking personal change—for example, the catalytic role of a negative performance appraisal or 360-degree assessment and the disconfirmation provided by a failure or personal disappointment. This frustration is the stick. When coupled with a carrot, such as strong personal ambition, a driving purpose, and a vision of our ideal selves, all the elements are in place for successful change. That's the theory, anyway.

The problem is that the carrot-and-stick theory of self-motivation rarely works, because change is so difficult. The statistics are depressing. Some 80 percent of people who make New Year's resolutions fall off the wagon by mid-February. Two-thirds of dieters gain back any lost weight within a year. Some people sign up for a year's gym membership and never show up; many stop after the first month. Seventy percent of coronary bypass patients revert to their unhealthy habits within two years of their operation.[7] Even in life-and-death situations, we're often resolutely resistant to change. We may know what we need to change and agree that it is desirable, but we find it hard to do anyhow.

Likewise, most managers seek a leadership course or coaching because of a stick (e.g., negative feedback from important stake-holders like their bosses) or a carrot (e.g., a desire to get promoted or increase their impact). But the managers still make little progress, because they lack a sense of urgency to do something about the feedback ("Yes, I need to lose weight and exercise more. I'll start next Monday").

Let's return to Jeff, whose team wrote "Solving problems" at the bottom of his Maslow pyramid of human needs (chapter 2). The negative performance appraisal he received for the first time ever, despite stellar results, didn't motivate him to change. Instead, he rationalized the negative feedback by explaining to his boss why it was a good thing for the company that he, Jeff, was such a micromanager.

So what did raise Jeff's urgency enough to put stepping up at the top of the priority list? It happened when his boss told him, "It's time for you to choose what path you want to follow. You are a valued manager, and we are expanding rapidly in the emerging markets. There will be many more operations for you to turn around, and you will be compensated handsomely. But if you want to eventually move into the senior leadership of this firm, you need to decide now, because which way you go determines your next assignment."

The tricky thing was that Jeff loved hands-on problem solving. But would he still love it so much after the nth time doing more or less the same? Jeff realized he would eventually get bored and find himself without other options. He concluded that the time to take action was now.

People like Jeff start to take the first steps only when they get this kind of now-or-never urgency. His urgency shot up when he realized that if he stayed too long in the same kind of role, he would never get a shot at the top. Other people experience an urgency infusion from meeting people who are clearly making a bigger impact or from one of the biggest urgency raisers of all—losing their job or an opportunity they really wanted.

Simple Addition

It's hard to stop doing something that is rewarding when there isn't a better, more interesting way to spend your time. That's why the best place to start is often by doing what I call *simple addition*: doing some new things that allow you to practice new behaviors and push you outside the box of your usual work routines and networks.

As described earlier in the book, Jacob never got around to delegating more and micromanaging less until he found something more interesting to do: working on his company's acquisition strategy. The problem, however, was that he was finding it hard to stick to his personal goal of spending two hours of uninterrupted time in his office, because every time he shut the door, one of his direct reports came knocking. They came knocking because he hadn't yet performed a second crucial operation: subtraction. He was still doing too much of the work himself.

As we saw, Jacob also resolved to patch up his relationship with his sales director and to get to know his peers across the lines better so that they were more likely to consider his ideas. After all, there was no use spending two hours a day thinking strategically if no one paid attention to his well-thought-out ideas. To increase his team's autonomy, Jacob also started investing more time coaching his subordinates and scheduling more meetings, to improve communication and detect problems earlier (and thus avoid the constant firefighting). He found himself busier than he had ever been.

Like Jacob, high achievers who start working on new skills typically find themselves with more things to do than there is time for. It's tough to squeeze new roles and activities into an already-full schedule, and our early efforts inevitably take time before they pay off enough that we willingly shed time-consuming tasks and responsibilities that no longer merit so much of our attention.[8] In the interim, our work continues to cue our old routines, and we find it hard to stick to the new plan. Only when the new leadership activity has become rewarding enough to be sustaining do people like Jacob stop investing large chunks of their time on the older, more ingrained operating habits.

Complication

Jacob had entered what I call the *complication stage*. He found himself reverting to his comfortable "driver" style, and his team concluded that his efforts to behave differently were not genuine.

Personal change, like organizational change, is rarely the linear, upward progression we naively hope it to be. (We assume that it's just a matter of getting hit by the right trigger or catalyst—or brick to the head.) Changing ourselves is also rarely the way theory tells us it should be—the familiar S curve with a slow takeoff followed by rapid progress past the tipping point. In fact, things usually get worse before they get better. Personal change is more like a line of peaks and valleys, false starts, new beginnings, rocky progress (figure 5-2).

We've already discussed one reason for the circuitous path to real change: your own capacity to stick with it through the harder times. A second reason is that many of the people around you

FIGURE 5-2

Models of personal change

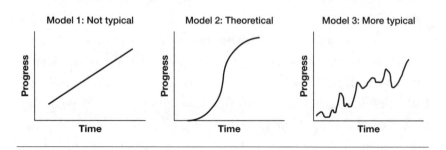

don't think you can or will sustain the changes—and that implicit expectation affects you much more than you'd think. Toward the end of my courses, when my students are feeling the most energized and motivated to go back to work and make some real changes, I show them a single-frame cartoon. In the background, a bespectacled man is bursting through an office door, arms raised in victory. He is wearing a superhero's cape and tights with "MANAGER'S EMPOWERMENT SEMINAR" emblazoned across his chest. Meanwhile in the foreground, a single worker, hunched over her desk and clutching her head, looks away and grimaces. Everyone laughs, but they get it.

The problem, as the cartoon illustrates, is that your newly inspired self inevitably returns to a team or an organization that does not understand or appreciate the new thinking to which you have been exposed. Your bosses, teams, close work colleagues, and even your friends and family haven't had the conversion experience. Worse, they will be suspicious of any new and unpredictable behavior on your part. Often, their attitude is, "If we just ignore him, he will get over it." Consciously or not, they remain invested in your old self. The pressures of the old situation conspire against your will to change, and soon, it's back to business as usual.

One financial services executive, Olav, fell exactly into this trap. He took a one-month-long general management course, as he needed a break from his longtime career with a firm he had helped to found. "I was burned out, unenthusiastic," he said. "I thought of taking the course as hitting the refresh button." During the training, Olav got excited by what he learned about leading change: "When I came back, I was pumped up to create change in my firm." But after a month away, his to-do list was long and everyone was eager for him to take care of what hadn't gotten done while he was away. The changes he looked forward to implementing failed to materialize.

Making progress through the complication stage often requires a new assignment, because staying in the old situation keeps you vulnerable to all the old expectations of the people who have come to know (and love) you in the old role. A new assignment is exactly what got Jeff through the transition. After he stepped up in the old job, his boss rewarded him with a stretch assignment: heading a larger unit that served a much larger market. This organization was way too big and complex to be run in Jeff's familiar, hands-on way, and although it needed improvement, it was not a turnaround. It forced him to do a very different job, to grow his network, and to change his sense of himself: it motivated him to take the change to the next level.

Course Correction

The frustration of the complication stage eventually led Olav to revisit his goals for himself. His training course had opened up a whole new world. He picked up exciting ideas about how to shake up his stodgy company. He met peers who shared similar experiences, and he was exposed to career paths he had never even envisioned. Before the program, he had simply wanted to refresh himself. But his ambitions grew as a result of everything he had experienced. An image of himself as someone who could more confidently take on a strategic role began to blossom. Unfortunately, neither his cofounder nor his subordinates were prepared for the metamorphosis; his fledgling efforts were stymied at each turn by a firm that hadn't grown as he had. On reflection, Olav realized he had outgrown the junior role his cofounder still expected him to play. Olav course-corrected his goals and ended up leaving to take an entrepreneurial path, starting his own firm.

Note that Olav's goals didn't guide his stepping-up process; they emerged from the process. He had not been clear about his objectives, simply because he himself did not previously know what they were. What good would it have done him to spend a lot of time up front getting clear on what his objectives were?[9]

How we set our objectives and how those goals help us perform are topics that have fascinated psychologists for decades.[10] Unfortunately, much advice to people in the midst of a transition comes down to mechanistic prescriptions, like setting specific, measurable, ambitious goals that presume a static world and leave little room for iteration. Most theories say, for example, that the most effective goals are concrete and measurable. But many times, our concrete goals don't take into account the likelihood that the new behaviors required to meet our goals will end up changing our objectives.

When the executives I teach come back to campus after months away working on the action commitments they made during the training, they typically return armed with different goals and concerns than those they had stated at the outset. After addressing the most problematic aspects of their 360-degree feedback, their other most urgent problems, and their personal goals that were the easiest to achieve, the executives start thinking about the medium to longer term. They also start thinking more about their own agendas, not just what other people want them to do.

This is when they begin to bring the outsight back in—to reflect, revise, and course-correct their goals for their careers and for themselves. In Olav's case, his frustration (and anger) ultimately led him to a deeper realization: he had outgrown his organization; in any case, it wasn't going to let him keep growing. This realization took a while to hit home because he was still operating under an older set of career and personal goals, ones that concerned his role in his current company.

While the changes we make at first begin with small steps and incremental moves, at some point it becomes important to reexamine the goals, priorities, and ambitions that have been driving us and to ask whether they are still relevant for the future. As we gain experience, we are better placed to judge our relative success or failure in meeting the goals we have previously set for ourselves and, more importantly, to step back to appraise whether our goals have changed.

Internalization

Psychologists use the term *internalization* to refer to the process by which superficial changes, tentative experiments, and fuzzy career goals become your own. I call it *bringing the outsight back in*. When you internalize a change, it becomes grounded—real and tangible—in your direct experience and is rooted in new self-definitions. The outsights become insights.

Internalization is the necessary step that allows people to move from what they know and do to who they are.[11] There is a big difference between doing what you think you are supposed to do and doing things because of who you are and what you firmly believe. For example, a manager might know that she has to deviate from her PowerPoint bullets to deliver a more emotional speech to badly demoralized employees and actually do a decent job of it. But if she has internalized the value of inspiring and connecting to people in a more personal way, she will deliver a more powerful speech because it is congruent with her values and her sense of the value she wants to bring: it's who she is. Likewise, it was one thing when I first told

FIGURE 5-3

The transition process

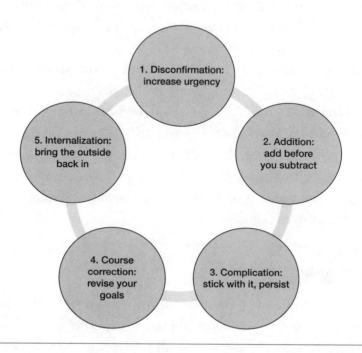

the story about being advised to "mark my territory" in class; it's quite another to appropriate it to make a point I now firmly believe.

Figure 5-3 summarizes the five stages of the transition process. It's a circle because, interestingly, becoming the kind of person you aspire to be is the most powerful motivator of all. This motivation will raise your urgency to keep going and seek out even more opportunities to lead. And the cycle begins again.

Stepping Up or Stepping Out?

In some instances, stepping up results in a move to a new assignment, as it did for Jeff. Alternatively, a person might stay in the same job but approach her work in a completely new and different way, as Sophie did. Other times, the journey leads us to a major career change, as it did for Olav.

How do we recognize when we have outgrown our jobs or organizations? When is it time to go? Many people who step up to leadership eventually get to this question, which is not always easy to answer. As we saw earlier, leadership experience increases clarity about who we are and want to become and creates urgency for more opportunities to develop our leadership further. When these motives remain unfulfilled by our organizations, we start to look elsewhere.

Many of the executives in this book ultimately asked themselves, "Should I stay or should I go?" For example, during her stint running alternative energy at BP, Vivienne Cox realized that her leadership style and philosophy had been evolving away from what she saw as the dominant model at her company. Her experiments with doing it more her way, within the context of a new venture within her organization, made her want to play around with her self-conception further. But the limits to what was possible within BP were hard and clear, and she ran up against them. So, she continued the work in a different role at another organization.

When a person reaches his midcareer, the stay-or-go question is often laden with psychological meaning, as it was for Robert (chapter 2), who ultimately realized that his motive for leaving wasn't just getting a bigger job. It was part of a growing-up process that required breaking free from his dysfunctional relationship with a father-figure boss and mentor whom Robert had never dared to oppose.

Having had a certain measure of career success, Robert, Vivienne, and many of the other managers whom I interviewed for this book came to ask themselves whether they wanted more of the same or something different, and whether their current organization allowed them sufficient rein to express the leader they had become. For anyone facing these kinds of questions, research on adult development suggests that making sense of the deeper outsights gained in the stepping-up process requires a more personal kind of reflection.[12]

A Life of Transitions

Psychologist Daniel Levinson is credited with having popularized the ideas of the seven-year itch and the midlife crisis. His research found that change tends to come in cycles and that lives evolve in alternating periods of stability and transition.

Stability periods, he said, lasted on average about seven years. That doesn't mean that we don't make any changes during these periods, and certainly, we make more frequent changes today than when Levinson first conducted his studies in the 1970s.[13] But the changes we make during these periods are more incremental. They don't upset everything. During a relatively stable period (relative because, of course, our lives are constantly evolving), we make a few key decisions regarding our work and family life, and these become the priorities around which we organize our lives and fit in (or leave out) everything else. Our job is to execute and implement "the plan." But after a while, we realize that something is not working in what we have set up. Maybe we've changed, maybe the situation has changed, and sometimes it's both.

During transition periods, which are shorter and typically last about three years, people become more open to reconsidering not just what they are doing but the premises and goals on which their actions are based. They consider, and often make, more radical changes. Our job now is to probe the choices we have made, explore alternative possibilities, and plant the seeds from which might grow a new period of relative stability.

The Big Questions

If you find yourself in a transitional period, it's probably because you've started doing some different things that give you a glimpse of new possibilities. That's when you need to step back and ask yourself questions like these:[a]

- What am I really getting from and giving to my work, colleagues, professional community—and myself?

- Do I know what I truly want for myself and others? How can I start finding out?

- What are my central values, and how are they reflected in my work?

- What are my greatest talents, and how am I using (or wasting) them?

- What have I done with my early ambitions, and what do I want of them now?

- Can I live my work life in a way that leaves enough room for other important facets of my life?

- How satisfactory is my present state and trajectory, and what changes can I make to provide a better basis for the future?

a. Daniel J. Levinson, *The Seasons of a Man's Life* (New York: Knopf, 1978), 192.

According to Levinson's research, the most potentially turbulent transition period of all happens sometime around age forty (many have argued, however, that today, fifty is the new forty because we are living and staying active longer).[14] At midlife or midcareer (however we may define it), people gain more urgency for change, seeing it as a now-or-never proposition. They feel that they still have enough time to play out another chapter of their lives or careers but not enough to waste time in an outdated one. They want to give rein to facets of themselves they have not had time to express. They also have enough experience with earlier choices to be able to evaluate them. And stuff happens that changes our priorities as well as the opportunities available. That's when we start asking the big questions (see the sidebar "The Big Questions").

One of the biggest challenges of a midcareer transition is knowing what to change and what to keep. Sometimes the temptation is to change everything at once. But major, external moves like changing jobs and careers won't always take us to a better place. James Marcia, a student of the great psychologist Erik Erickson, argued that what is more important instead is to grow by questioning where we are today, actively entertaining alternatives, and eventually committing to making changes, whether they are external changes like job moves or more internal changes like changing the way we think about what we do and why.[15]

His model of the different "identity states" that can characterize a person at any given moment is summarized in figure 5-4. Each of the four states describes where a person falls along two continua: exploration on the one hand and commitment to concrete choices on the other. When we commit to a career path, job, or company without ever exploring whether it is the right choice for us, we *foreclose* on options that might be more rewarding (quadrant 1). If we don't yet commit but continue to explore, such as taking a sabbatical, going back to school for a spell, or even job hopping in search of ourselves, we are in what Marcia calls the *moratorium* stage (quadrant 2). But when we question endlessly without truly exploring anything in depth and never commit to an old or a new career path, we also forgo the possibility of mastery and maturity. Marcia calls this stage *identity diffusion* (quadrant 3), because we are figuratively all over the place. As one person I interviewed put it, "There are two types of people. Some are always jumping. Some never jump—they settle down too easily and get stuck." To be a growing adult means making commitments that are informed by prior exploration and questioning (quadrant 4); this stage is *identity achievement*, an apt term because it only comes to us through a process of becoming ourselves.

The problem with what Marcia calls foreclosure is that we often don't realize that's what we are doing. No one chooses to foreclose options explicitly. But that's what happens when we let the years elapse without asking ourselves the big questions. Too much certainty is as much a problem as too much doubt, not necessarily because we might be in the wrong job but because we might unwittingly remain the victim of other people's values and expectations. Sometimes we so fully internalize what other people think is right for us that we don't ever become what Harvard psychologist Robert Kegan calls "self-authoring."[16] Earlier

---

FIGURE 5-4

The four states of exploration and commitment in managing transitions

		Commitment	
		Present	Absent
Exploration	Present	Achievement: Become your own person (quadrant 4)	Moratorium: Take a time out, suspend decisions (quadrant 2)
	Absent	Foreclosure: Foreclose options (quadrant 1)	Diffusion: Remain indefinitely without a clear identity or career commitment (quadrant 3)

Source: Adapted from J. E. Marcia, "Development and Validation of Ego Identity Status," *Journal of Personality and Social Psychology* 3 (1966): 551–558.

Self-Assessment:
Are You in a Career-Building Period
or in a Career-Transitioning Period?

	YES	NO
1. I have been in the same job, career path, or organization for at least seven years.		
2. I find myself feeling a bit restless professionally.		
3. On balance, my job is more draining than energizing.		
4. I resent not having more time for my outside interests or family.		
5. My family configuration is changing in ways that free me up to explore different options; for example, my kids have left for college or my partner's career situation has changed.		
6. I envy (or admire) the people around me who have made major professional changes.		

in our lives and careers, Kegan explains, we make decisions according to social expectations about what constitutes a good job, a good employer, and a loyal employee. The task at midcareer is to understand those hidden assumptions so that we can break free from our "ought selves"—what important people in our lives think we ought to be—to become our own person. The sidebar

	YES	NO
7. My work has lost some of its meaning for me.	_____	_____
8. I find that my career ambitions are changing.	_____	_____
9. Recent personal events (e.g., a health scare, the death of a loved one, the birth of a child, marriage, or divorce) have led me to reappraise what I really want.	_____	_____
10. I don't jump out of bed in the morning excited about the upcoming day.	_____	_____

Assess whether you are in a transitional period by totaling the number of "yes" responses:

6–10   You are likely to be deep into a career-transitioning period. Make time to reflect not only on your new experiences but also on whether your life goals and priorities need rethinking.

3–5   You may be entering a career-transitioning period. Work to increase outsight via new activities and relationships.

2 or below   You are more likely to be in a career-building period.

"Self-Assessment: Are You in a Career-Building Period or in a Career-Transitioning Period?" can help you understand where you are in a transition.

The process of bringing the outsight back in might lead you to make significant external changes in your career and lifestyle; alternatively, you may entertain doubts but decide to remain where you are, making changes that can be significant even if they are not so visible to the outside world. The stepping-up process outlined in this chapter describes the path to getting there.

CHAPTER 5 SUMMARY

✓ Stepping up to play a bigger leadership role is not an event; it's a process that takes time before it pays off. It is a transition built from small changes.

✓ Most methods for changing ask you to begin with the end in mind—the desired outcome. But in reality, knowing what kind of leader you want to become comes last, not first, in the stepping-up process.

✓ The transition process is rarely linear; difficulties and complications will inevitably arise and often follow a predictable sequence of five stages:
   1. Disconfirmation
   2. Simple addition
   3. Complication
   4. Course correction
   5. Internalization

✓ Getting unstuck when problems inevitably arise requires that you reflect and integrate the new learning—to bring the outsight back in—so that the ensuing changes are driven by a new self-image that is based on your direct experience.

✓ Making major, external moves like changing jobs and careers, however, does not necessarily take you to a better place. More important is to grow by questioning where you are today, actively entertaining alternatives, and eventually committing to making changes. The changes can be external, like job moves, or more internal, like changing the way you think about what you do and why.

✓ Breaking free from your "ought self"—what important people in your life think you ought to be—is at the heart of the transition process.

Act Now

NO MATTER WHAT YOU ARE DOING TODAY, chances are that you are facing some kind of do-it-yourself transition. That means you are not only responsible for your own development (as we all are) but also need to know when it's time to start stepping up to leadership even if there's no new assignment on the horizon. If you don't create new opportunities even within the confines of your current job, the next assignment, promotion, or career stage may never come your way.

Where do you begin? Probably the most important lesson in this book is that the only way to become a leader is to act like one. Action—changing how you do your job, how you build and use your network, and how you express yourself—gives you outsight, the fresh, external perspective you need to understand more deeply what is involved in the work of leadership and to motivate yourself to do it. Outsight holds the power to reshape your image of who you are, what you can do, and what is worth doing—it will change the way you think. You'll remake yourself as you grow and the world changes.

A point worth underlining: everyone around you will tell you that to be a better leader, you need to self-reflect, introspect, know what you want, increase self-awareness. All of that is well and good, but it will only help you later, when you have some new experiences to reflect on. Otherwise, all your material for reflection is the outdated past. Insight is an outcome, not an input.

Knowing the kind of leader you'd like to become is not the starting point on your development journey, but rather the result of increasing your outsight. You must reverse the conventional "thinking before doing" logic to successfully step up.

Making a leap from a lifetime of expert contributions and hands-on control to the more subtle processes of thinking strategically, working through networks, and leading more authentically is not a one-shot deal, and it does not happen overnight. The transition is built from small changes, is less than linear, and is distinctly uncomfortable. It will take time before you achieve the results you want. The process is full of complications, false starts, setbacks, and unanticipated turns, but the mess of it all sets the stage for more profound internal changes. At some point, we have to start bringing the outsight back in, connecting the dots among our new leadership experiences to reflect on what they mean for us, our work, and career.

New ways of acting not only change how we think—our perspective on what is important and worth doing—but also change who we become. We start by doing, we reflect on our experience, and we rethink ourselves. Whether we decide to take the leap to a new company or a different career or conclude that it's better to stay on the current path, all of us struggle with crafting a work role in which we feel both part of something larger (the organization, the work) and free enough to be ourselves. Through reflecting on our new experiences, we can better know and pursue our own aims—what the Irish philosopher and author Charles Handy called creating "a life of our own."[1]

My Own Leadership Transition

A little over ten years ago, I was dragged kicking and screaming into a new leadership job, a three-year tour of duty as chair of my department at INSEAD. As a lifelong academic, I enjoy writing and researching; I believe I do well at it, and I have been rewarded for it. It was one thing to teach leadership, but quite another to actually have to practice it. Maddeningly, the new role took so much time away from what I really wanted to do and thought I did best: write my books and articles.

I remember feeling more and more frustrated during my first year in the job. The task at hand was guiding my group to define its strategic priorities. That meant having to do all the things I teach: setting a direction, communicating priorities, getting buy-in from key stakeholders inside and outside the group, and having meetings—meetings before the meeting, meetings after the meeting, one-on-one meetings, informal small-group meetings—and so on. But still no one agreed. My new leadership position was exhausting and was putting a big dent in my publication record. I wasn't happy.

I remember vividly a department meeting that took place about one year into the job. I had spent much time over the previous twelve months trying to get consensus on some key issues. To my dismay, I found myself having an almost identical conversation with the same people, who were repeating more or less the same things that they had said one year earlier. And I remember saying to myself, "With all the time I have put into this, I could have written one or two new articles, and at least I would have had a clear payoff for the time I invested."

Then I realized that I was exactly in the same boat as the executives I was teaching. I wasn't stepping up to leadership, because I didn't think that leading was real work. Therefore, I wasn't investing enough time doing it to see a payoff from my investment. With no results for my efforts, the sacrifice of so much of my precious "doing" time would never seem worthwhile. If it didn't seem worthwhile, I wasn't going to do much more than comply with the minimum job requirements: scheduling, holding and attending meetings, assigning people and groups to tasks, managing performance appraisals, staffing courses, mentoring the junior faculty on their teaching and research, conducting performance reviews, fighting fires when conflicts erupted, and maybe organizing occasional social events around promotions, retirements, and holidays. You get the picture: I wasn't leading anything. I found the job draining.

Stepping up to leadership, as was true in my case, rarely means eliminating everything else we used to do. Instead, it requires us to make delicate judgments about how to reallocate our time—what to do less of, what to do more of, and what new activities to add. What happens invariably is that we try to keep most of the old things we liked to do and were rewarded for, add the obvious new responsibilities (which are often the least fun, because they tend to be imposed by others), and neglect to think strategically about what new activities we need to add to make the job our own.

In my case, my limited view of the job was negatively self-reinforcing. Instead of driving an agenda of things I wanted to accomplish, I stayed in reactive mode, doing the least rewarding of the administrative tasks. Worse, other people's agendas somehow ended up on my plate—some of the things I spent the most time and energy on had very little bearing on my effectiveness as a group leader. And because I was so pressed for time, the last thing that would have occurred to me was to spend time outside my area, where I could hang out with other colleagues or volunteer for committees or task forces. I was even limiting my external activities—and these are the lifeblood of academic careers—more than I ever had, because I was so worried about my individual productivity. Naturally, my whole view of who I was and how I could best contribute was at odds with my responsibilities of leading the group.

Four years ago, when I started working on this book, I was asked again to lead my group for another three-year term.

This time I did it gladly, with personal enjoyment, and I am proud of what I accomplished. I worked less hard (and had more time to write), but my work was very focused on a couple of key priorities that I focused on single-mindedly. They involved growing my group and removing the single most obvious barriers to my group's ability to recruit the best faculty and then let the faculty members get on with their research—a practice that helped us get them promoted instead of losing them after so much investment. Pretty much anything else was delegated or ignored.

A colleague of mine, a neophyte, once confessed to me that he found the job of leading draining. Funnily enough, he is a leadership researcher. I asked him what he thought about the job. He answered me according to popular theory: "You have to have a clear purpose for doing this." For him, it was all about service to his group members. "That's a lofty goal," I said, "but service for what?" He was serving left and right with no clear agenda of his own about what mattered most and what key levers would make the biggest impact.

What changed for me? Many things. In the time between the two appointments, several committees and task forces I was involved with at the school gave me a bigger-picture view of how the different pieces of the institution worked and helped me get to know colleagues outside my area better. I took some different roles outside INSEAD and served on Harvard Business School's Visiting Committee. I sat on some advisory boards and started working with the World Economic Forum on its leadership program, the annual conference at Davos, and its global agenda councils. My professional relationships expanded way beyond my traditional academic connections. I found my new activities so interesting that I was motivated to spend less time on the things I didn't find so rewarding.

I could go on, but you get the point. I had acted my way into a new way of thinking about leading.

Connecting the Dots

In his famous Stanford graduation speech, Steve Jobs talked about things he did as an undergraduate dropout, such as taking a calligraphy course that would profoundly affect the look and feel of Apple products many years later. He never expected that this side interest of his would have such profound consequences for his later achievements. "You can't connect the dots looking forward; you can only connect them looking backwards," he concluded.[2]

Like Jobs, you may not see at first how all the dots connect as you start branching out beyond your routine work, habitual networks, and historical ways of defining yourself. You won't know where it's all going to take you. But these new ways of acting will slowly change the way you think about your work and yourself, giving you fresh material for reflection and urging you on to find more meaningful ways of leading at work and in your life beyond.

Slowly but surely, a more central and enduring leader identity starts to takes root, one that motivates you to spend more time "doing leadership," expands the pool of people you learn and draw inspiration from, and eventually raises the level of enjoyment and sense of competency you derive from it. In time, it will influence your choice of activities and settings, as you will be prone to invest in those that increase your capacity to provide leadership. Sometimes the journey leads to a major career shift; other times, the transition is internal: you've changed the way you see your work and yourself.

It's worth it. Start now. Act now.

Notes

Chapter 1

1. The name *Jacob* is a pseudonym. To ensure anonymity, I used pseudonyms for all participants in my research studies. In addition, particular details of their lives, such as where they live or where they worked before the career change, have been altered somewhat. I use real names when I am citing from public sources.

2. Some examples of this approach include Marcus Buckingham and Donald O. Clifton, *Now, Discover Your Strengths* (New York: Free Press, 2001); James M. Kouzes and Barry Z. Posner, *The Leadership Challenge: How to Make Extraordinary Things Happen in Organizations* (San Francisco: Jossey-Bass, 2012); Bill George, *Authentic Leadership: Rediscovering the Secrets to Creating Lasting Value* (San Francisco: Jossey-Bass, 2004).

3. The "do good, be good" idea comes from Aristotle's statement "These virtues are formed in man by his doing the actions" (*The Nicomachean Ethics*), summarized as "We are what we repeatedly do," in Will Durant, *The Story of Philosophy: The Lives and Opinions of the World's Greatest Philosophers* (New York: Simon & Schuster, 1926).

4. Thinking follows action: self-perception theory posits that people infer their attributes by observing their freely chosen actions. See Daryl J. Bem, "Self-Perception: An Alternative Interpretation of Cognitive Dissonance Phenomena," *Psychological Review* 74, no. 3 (1967): 183–200.

5. Richard T. Pascale, Mark Millemann, and Linda Gioja, "Changing the Way We Change," *Harvard Business Review* 75, no. 6 (1997): 126–139. Richard T. Pascale, Mark Millemann and Linda Gioja, *Surfing the Edge of Chaos: The Laws of Nature and the New Laws of Business* (New York: Crown Business, 2001).

6. David A. Jopling, *Self-Knowledge and the Self* (New York: Routledge, 2000).

7. D. Scott DeRue and Susan J. Ashford, "Who Will Lead and Who Will Follow? A Social Process of Leadership Identity Construction in Organizations," *Academy of Management Review* 35, no. 4 (2010): 627–647; Herminia Ibarra, Sarah Wittman, Gianpiero Petriglieri, and David V. Day, "Leadership and Identity: An Examination of Three Theories and New Research Directions," in *The Oxford Handbook of Leadership and Organizations*, ed. David V. Day (New York: Oxford University Press, 2014).

8. Karl E. Weick, *Sensemaking in Organizations* (Thousand Oaks, CA: Sage Publications, 1995).

9. Survey of 173 INSEAD executive students conducted in October 2013. Of the 173 participants, 80 percent were men and 20 percent were women; this matches the gender split of the population. The average age of the participants was 42.1 years. Of the participants, 46 percent were employed in general management functions with profit-and-loss responsibility, 31 percent were in functional management (e.g., marketing), and 12 percent were in project or team management. See Marshall Goldsmith and Mark Reiter, *What Got You Here Won't Get You There: How Successful People Become Even More Successful* (New York: Hyperion, 2007).

10. Some of my early work on authenticity dilemmas is Herminia Ibarra, "Making Partner: A Mentor's Guide to the Psychological Journey," *Harvard Business Review* 78, no. 2 (2000): 146–155; Herminia Ibarra, "Provisional Selves: Experimenting with Image and Identity in Professional Adaptation," *Administrative Science Quarterly* 44, no. 4 (1999): 764–791. For my research on career change, see Herminia Ibarra, *Working Identity: Unconventional Strategies for Reinventing Your Career* (Boston: Harvard Business School Publishing, 2003); and Herminia Ibarra, "How to Stay Stuck in the Wrong Career," *Harvard Business Review* 80, no. 12 (2002): 40–48. For a discussion of leader development as identity change, see Herminia Ibarra, Scott A. Snook, and Laura Guillén Ramo, "Identity-Based Leader Development," in *Handbook of Leadership Theory and Practice*, ed. Nitin Nohria and Rakesh Khurana (Boston: Harvard Business Press, 2010).

11. Some of my early research on networks includes Herminia Ibarra and Steven B. Andrews, "Power, Social Influence and Sense Making: Effects of Network Centrality and Proximity on Employee Perceptions," *Administrative Science Quarterly* 38, no. 2 (1993): 277–303; and Herminia Ibarra, "Network Centrality, Power and Innovation Involvement: Determinants of Technical and Administrative Roles," *Academy of Management Journal* 36, no. 3 (1993): 471–501. A more recent discussion for a managerial audience is Herminia Ibarra and Mark Hunter, "How Leaders Create and Use Networks," *Harvard Business Review* 85, no. 1 (2007): 40–47.

12. See, for example, Jon R. Katzenbach and Zia Khan, *Leading Outside the Lines: How to Mobilize the Informal Organization, Energize Your Team, and Get Better Results* (San Francisco: Jossey-Bass, 2010); Chris Ernst and Donna Chrobot-Mason, *Boundary Spanning Leadership: Six Practices for Solving Problems, Driving Innovation, and Transforming Organizations* (New York: McGraw-Hill, 2010); and Herminia Ibarra and Morten T. Hansen, "Are You a Collaborative Leader?" *Harvard Business Review* 89, nos. 7–8 (2011): 68–74.

13. For a comprehensive treatment of each of the transitions managers encounter as they move up the leadership pipeline, see Ram Charan, Stephen Drotter, and James Noel, *The Leadership Pipeline: How to Build the Leadership Powered Company* (San Francisco: Jossey-Bass, 2011); Markus Hazel and Paula Nurius, "Possible Selves," *American Psychologist* 41, no. 9 (1986): 954–969; and Linda A. Hill, *Becoming a Manager* (Boston: Harvard Business School Publishing, 2003).

14. Jeffrey Pfeffer and Robert I. Sutton, *The Knowing-Doing Gap: How Smart Companies Turn Knowledge into Action* (Boston: Harvard Business School Publishing, 2000); David H. Maister, *Strategy and the Fat Smoker: Doing What's Obvious but Not Easy* (Boston: The Spangle Press, 2008).

15. Ronald A. Heifetz, *Leadership Without Easy Answers* (Cambridge, MA: Belknap Press of Harvard University Press, 1994).

16. Joel M. Podolny, Rakesh Khurana, and Marya Hill-Popper, "Revisiting the Meaning of Leadership," in *Handbook of Leadership Theory and Practice*, ed. Nitin Nohria and Rakesh Khurana (Boston: Harvard Business Press, 2010).

17. John P. Kotter, *Power and Influence* (New York: Free Press, 2008).

18. Jack Welch quoted in *Inc.* (March 1995): 13.

Chapter 2

1. For the classic study of how companies fall into competency traps, see Clayton M. Christensen, *The Innovator's Dilemma: When New Technologies Cause Great Firms to Fail* (Boston: Harvard Business School Publishing: 1997). For how people fall into competency traps, see Marshall Goldsmith and Mark Reiter, *What Got You Here Won't Get You There: How Successful People Become Even More Successful* (New York: Hyperion, 2007); and Mark E. Van Buren and Todd Safferstone, "The Quick Wins Paradox," *Harvard Business Review* 87, no. 1 (2009): 54–61.

2. Goldsmith and Reiter, *What Got You Here.*

3. For the classic work on self-efficacy, see Albert Bandura, *Self-Efficacy: The Exercise of Control* (New York: Worth Publishers, 1997).

4. Maslow's hierarchy of needs is a theory in psychology described in Abraham H. Maslow, "A Theory of Human Motivation," *Psychological Review* 50, no. 4 (1943): 370–396.

5. The difference between exploiting current competencies and exploring to gain new competencies is a classic trade-off in corporate strategy and individual learning. See James G. March, "Exploration and Exploitation in Organizational Learning," *Organization Science* 2, no. 1 (1991): 71–87.

6. The classic distinction was first developed by Abraham Zaleznik and popularized by John P. Kotter. Abraham Zaleznik, "Managers and Leaders: Are They Different?" *Harvard Business Review* 55 (May–June 1977): 67–78; and John P. Kotter, *A Force for Change: How Leadership Differs from Management* (New York: Free Press, 1990).

7. Deborah Ancona and Henrik Bresman, *X-Teams: How to Build Teams That Lead, Innovate and Succeed* (Boston: Harvard Business School Publishing, 2007). The original research leading to this insight is Deborah Ancona and David F Caldwell, "Bridging the Boundary: External Activity and Performance in Organizational Teams," *Administrative Science Quarterly* 37, no. 4 (1992): 634–665.

8. Although BP eventually took a turn away from alternative energy under Tony Hayward's tenure as CEO, the organization Cox built remains and continues to develop energy alternatives for BP. Herminia Ibarra and Mark Hunter, "Vivienne Cox at BP Alternative Energy", Case 5473 (Fontainebleau: INSEAD, October 2007).

9. Ibid.

10. Herminia Ibarra and Cristina Escallon, "Jack Klues: Managing Partner VivaKi (C)", Case 5643 (Fontainebleau: INSEAD, December 2009).

11. James M. Kouzes and Barry Z. Posner, "To Lead, Create a Shared Vision," *Harvard Business Review* 87, no. 1 (2009).

12. James M. Kouzes and Barry Z. Posner, *The Leadership Challenge: How to Make Extraordinary Things Happen in Organizations* (San Francisco: Jossey-Bass, 2012); Burt Nanus, *Visionary Leadership* (San Francisco: Jossey-Bass, 1995).

13. Roger L. Martin, "The Big Lie of Strategic Planning?" *Harvard Business Review* 92, nos. 1–2 (2014): 78–84; Roger L. Martin, "Are You Confusing Strategy with Planning?" *Harvard Business Review Blog*, May 2, 2014; Roger L. Martin, "Why Smart People Struggle with Strategy," *Harvard Business Review Blog*, June 12, 2014.

14. Manfred F. R. Kets de Vries, Pierre Vrignaud, Elizabeth Florent-Treacy and Konstantin Korotov, "360-degree feedback instrument: An overview," *INSEAD Working Paper*, 2007. My research indicates that while

everyone falls short on envisioning, women are more likely than men to rate a shortfall on this dimension. See Herminia Ibarra and Otilia Obodaru, "Women and the Vision Thing," *Harvard Business Review* 87, no. 1 (2009): 62–70.

15. Amy J. C. Cuddy, Matthew Kohut, and John Neffinger, "Connect, Then Lead," *Harvard Business Review* 91, nos. 7–8 (2013): 54–61.

16. Jay A. Conger and Rabindra N. Kanungo, *Charismatic Leadership in Organizations* (Thousand Oaks, CA: SAGE Publications, 1998).

17. James R. Meindl, "The Romance of Leadership as a Follower-Centric Theory: A Social Constructionist Approach," *Leadership Quarterly* 6, no. 3 (1995): 329–341; and Rob Goffee and Gareth Jones, *Why Should Anyone Be Led by You? What It Takes to Be an Authentic Leader* (Boston: Harvard Business School Publishing, 2006).

18. Herminia Ibarra and Jennifer M. Suesse, "Margaret Thatcher," Case 497018 (Boston: Harvard Business School, revised May 13, 1998).

19. Herminia Ibarra and Cristina Escallon, "David Kenny: Managing Partner VivaKi (B)," Case 5643 (Fontainebleau: INSEAD, December 2009).

20. Melba Duncan, "The Case for Executive Assistants," *Harvard Business Review*, 89, no. 5 (2011).

21. Sheryl Sandberg, *Lean In: Women, Work, and the Will to Lead* (New York: Knopf, 2013), ch. 4. For the last few years, the research organization Catalyst has been surveying MBA graduates from top business schools to understand what career pathways lead to greater success. They found that 62 percent of the people they surveyed described obtaining stretch and high-profile assignments as having the greatest impact on their careers.

22. TED is a nonprofit devoted to spreading ideas under the slogan "Ideas Worth Spreading." The format is usually short (eighteen minutes or shorter) talks. For an explanation of the TED format, see Chris Anderson, "How to Give a Killer Presentation," *Harvard Business Review* 91, no. 6 (2013): 121–125; and Jeremey Donovan, *How to Deliver a TED Talk: Secrets of the World's Most Inspiring Presentations* (New York: McGraw-Hill, 2013).

23. Joseph L. Badaracco, *Defining Moments: When Managers Must Choose Between Right and Right* (Boston: Harvard Business School Publishing, 1997), 58–61; Herminia Ibarra and R. Barbulescu, "Identity as Narrative: A Process Model of Narrative Identity Work in Macro Work Role Transition," *Academy of Management Review* 35, no. 1 (2010): 135–154.

24. See, for example, Annette Simmons, *Whoever Tells the Best Story Wins: How to Use Your Own Stories to Communicate with Power and Impact* (New York: AMACOM, 2007).

25. Annette Simmons, "The Six Stories You Need to Know How to Tell," in *The Story Factor* (New York: Basic Books, 2006).

26. John P. Kotter, "What Effective General Managers Really Do," *Harvard Business Review* 77, no. 2 (1999): 145–159.

27. Sendhil Mullainathan and Eldar Shafir, *Scarcity: Why Having Too Little Means So Much* (New York: Times Books, 2013).

28. The classic text on how to make room for what is important but not urgent is Stephen R. Covey, *The 7 Habits of Highly Effective People: Powerful Lessons in Personal Change* (New York: Free Press, 2004).

Chapter 3

1. For a review of the research on how networks affect careers, see Herminia Ibarra and Prashant H. Deshpande, "Networks and Identities: Reciprocal Influences on Career Processes and Outcomes," in *The Handbook of Career Studies*, ed. Maury Peiperl and Hugh Gunz (Thousand Oaks, CA: SAGE Publications, 2007), 268–283.

2. Herminia Ibarra, "Network Assessment Exercise: Executive Version," Case 497003 (Boston: Harvard Business School, revised July 31, 2008).

3. This research is summarized in Miller McPherson, Lynn Smith-Lovin, and James M. Cook, "Birds of a Feather: Homophily in Social Networks," *Annual Review of Sociology* 27, no. 1 (2001): 415–444. In research jargon, the *narcissism principle* is called *homophily*, the tendency for discretionary relationships to form among people who share a common status or social identity. Research on the prevalence of homophily in social relationships also shows why it can be so hard to network professionally across race and gender lines. See, for example, Herminia Ibarra, "Homophily and Differential Returns: Sex Differences in Network Structure and Access in an Advertising Firm," *Administrative Science Quarterly* 37, no. 3 (1992): 422–447.

4. See, for example, Nigel Nicholson, *Executive Instinct: Managing the Human Animal in the Information Age* (New York: Crown Business, 2000). Nicholson says that only by acknowledging that our brains are "hardwired" for survival can we understand behavior and "manage" our instincts.

5. Monica J. Harris and Christopher P. Garris, in *First Impressions*, ed. Nalini Ambady and John J. Skowronski (New York, NY: Guilford Publications), 147–168.

6. The propinquity effect is a concept proposed by psychologists Leon Festinger, Stanley Schachter, and Kurt Back to explain that the more frequently we interact with people, the more likely we are to form friendships

and romantic relationships with them. In a 1950 study carried out in the Westgate student apartments on the campus of Massachusetts Institute of Technology the authors tracked friendship formation among couples in graduate housing; the closer together people lived, even within a building, the more likely they were to become close friends. Leon Festinger, Stanley Schachter, and Kurt Back, "The Spatial Ecology of Group Formation," in *Social Pressure in Informal Groups: A Study of Human Factors in Housing*, ed. Leon Festinger, Stanley Schachter, and Kurt Back (Stanford, CA: Stanford University Press, 1963).

7. Ibid. The propinquity effect works due to mere exposure, i. e., the more exposure we have to a stimulus, the more apt we are to like it, provided the stimulus is not noxious.

8. Stanley Milgram, "The Small-World Problem," *Psychology Today* 1, no. 1 (1967): 61–67.

9. Nicholas A. Christakis and James H. Fowler, "The Spread of Obesity in a Large Social Network over 32 Years," *New England Journal of Medicine* 357, no. 4 (2007): 370–379. See also their book, *Connected: The Surprising Power of Our Social Networks and How They Shape Our Lives* (New York: Little, Brown and Co., 2009).

10. This number comes from Morten Hansen, "The Search Transfer Problem: The Role of Weak Ties in Sharing Knowledge Across Organization Subunits," *Administrative Science Quarterly* 44, no. 1 (1999).

11. Individuals' mobility is enhanced when they have a large, sparse network of informal ties for acquiring information and resources. But since stakeholder expectations may diverge, they also benefit from a consistency of messages they get from a dense core of key people who agree on what they should be doing. Joel M. Podolny and James N. Baron "Resources and Relationships: Social Networks and Mobility in the Workplace," *American Sociological Review* 62, no. 5 (1997): 673–693.

12. Boris Groysberg and Deborah Bell, "Case Study: Should a Female Director 'Tone It Down'?" *Harvard Business Review Blog*, July 29, 2014.

13. James D. Westphal and Laurie P. Milton, "How Experience and Network Ties Affect the Influence of Demographic Minorities on Corporate Boards," *Administrative Science Quarterly* 45, no. 2 (2000): 366–398.

14. Malcom Gladwell, *The Tipping Point: How Little Things Can Make a Big Difference* (Boston: Back Bay Books, 2002).

15. Joel M. Podolny and James N. Baron, "Resources and Relationships: Social Networks and Mobility in the Workplace," *American Sociological Review* 62, no. 5 (1997): 673–693.

16. Sociologist Mark Granovetter examined the importance of weak ties in his classic 1974 book *Getting a Job*, in which he found that most people obtained their jobs through acquaintances, not close friends. Mark S. Granovetter, *Getting a Job: A Study of Contacts and Careers*, 2nd ed. (Chicago: University of Chicago Press, 1995). See also Mark S. Granovetter, "The Strength of Weak Ties," *American Journal of Sociology* 78, no. 6 (1973): 1360–1380.

17. Etienne Wenger, *Communities of Practice: Learning, Meaning, and Identity* (New York: Cambridge University Press, 1998). Wenger coined the phrase *communities of practice* to describe groups that share a common body of professional expertise and identify as members of that community.

18. Using a Facebook database that included 950 million people, Eman Yasser Daraghmi and Shyan-Ming Yuan showed that the average number of acquaintances separating any two people, even those who work in rare jobs, is not 6 but 3.9. "We are so close, less than 4 degrees separating you and me!" *Computers in Human Behavior* 30 (January 2014): 273–285.

19. Patrick Reynolds, "The Oracle of Bacon," website, accessed August 27, 2014, http://oracleofbacon.org/.

20. LinkedIn founder Reid Hoffman makes this point well. See Reid Hoffman and Ben Casnocha, *The Start-Up of You: Adapt to the Future, Invest in Yourself, and Transform Your Career* (New York: Crown Business, 2012): 110–115.

21. Kathleen L. McGinn and Nicole Tempest, "Heidi Roizen," Case 800-228 (Boston: Harvard Business School, January 2000; revised April 2010); Ken Auletta, "A Woman's Place: Can Sheryl Sandberg Upend Silicon Valley's Male-Dominated Culture?" *The New Yorker*, July 11, 2011.

22. Chris's story is told in more detail in Peter Killing, "Nestle's Globe Program," Cases IMD-3-1334, IMD-3-1334, IMD-3-1336 (Lausanne, Switzerland: IMD, January 1, 2003).

23. Judith Rich Harris, *The Nurture Assumption: Why Children Turn Out the Way They Do* (New York: Free Press; updated edition, 2009), explains how and why the tendency of children to take cues from their peers (and not their parents) works to their evolutionary advantage.

24. David Brooks, "Bill Wilson's Gospel," *New York Times*, June 28, 2010. See also David Brooks, *The Social Animal: The Hidden Sources of Love, Character, and Achievement* (New York: Random House, 2011), 270–271.

25. For an accessible review of research on the power of reference groups, see Harris, *The Nurture Assumption*.

26. Steven Johnson, *Where Good Ideas Come From* (New York: Riverhead Trade; reprint 2011).

Chapter 4

1. To use the phrase popularized by Harvard Business School professor and former Medtronic CEO Bill George, in Bill George and Peter Sims, *True North: Discover Your Authentic Leadership* (San Francisco: Jossey-Bass, 2007).

2. There are more than twenty thousand books with the word *authentic* in the title on Amazon.com.

3. People born between 1957 and 1964 held an average of 11.3 jobs between age eighteen and forty-six (US Bureau of Labor Statistics, *Number of Jobs Held, Labor Market Activity, and Earnings Growth Among the Youngest Baby Boomers*, July 25, 2012). On the "protean career," see Douglas T. Hall, "Self-Awareness, Identity, and Leader Development," in *Leader Development for Transforming Organizations: Growing Leaders for Tomorrow*, ed. David V. Day, Stephen J. Zaccaro, and Stanley M. Halpin (Mahwah, NJ: Laurence Erlbaum Associates, 2004): 153–176.

4. Mark Snyder, *Public Appearances, Private Realities: The Psychology of Self-Monitoring* (New York: W. H. Freeman, 1987).

5. Martin Kilduff and David V. Day, "Do Chameleons Get Ahead? The Effects of Self-Monitoring on Managerial Careers," *Academy of Management Journal* 37, no. 4 (1994): 1047–1060.

6. For how tacit knowledge is shared, see Ikujiro Nonaka, "A Dynamic Theory of Organizational Knowledge Creation," *Organization Science* 5, no. 1 (1994): 14–37.

7. E. Tory Higgins, "Promotion and Prevention: Regulatory Focus as a Motivational Principle" in *Advances in Experimental Social Psychology*, ed. Mark P. Zanna (San Diego: Academic Press, 1998): 1–46.

8. "Properly speaking, a man has as many social selves as there are individuals who recognize him and carry an image of him in their mind . . . [W]e may practically say that he has as many different social selves as there are distinct groups of persons about whose opinion he cares. He generally shows a different side of himself to each of these different groups." William James, *The Principles of Psychology*, vol. 1 (New York: Henry Holt & Co., 1890; repr., New York: Dover Publications, 1950), 294.

9. Hazel Markus and Paula Nurius, "Possible Selves," *American Psychologist* 41, no. 9 (1986): 954–969.

10. I'm grateful to Claudio Fernández-Aráoz for passing on this insight, which he got from Egon Zehnder's chairman, Damien O'Brien.

11. In this usage, authenticity conveys moral meaning about one's values and choices. A person, for instance, is said to be authentic if he is sincere, assumes responsibility for his actions, and makes explicit value-based choices concerning those actions and appearances rather than accepting pre-programmed or socially imposed values and actions.

12. See Bruce J. Avolio and William L. Gardner, "Authentic Leadership Development: Getting to the Root of Positive Forms of Leadership," *Leadership Quarterly* 16, no. 3 (2005): 315–333; and George and Sims, *True North*.

13. Robert G. Lord and Rosalie J. Hall, "Identity, Deep Structure and the Development of Leadership Skill," *Leadership Quarterly* 16, no. 4 (2005): 591–615, argue that a new leader's central concern is emulating leadership behaviors to project an image of himself or herself as a leader that others will validate and reward. Expert leaders develop an increasing capacity to pursue internally held values and personalized strategies in service of goals that include others.

14. In light of her research in psychology, Susan Cain, *Quiet: The Power of Introverts in a World That Can't Stop Talking* (New York: Broadway Books, 2013), explains how introverts are capable of behaving like extroverts when it is in the service of a purpose that matters to them.

15. A person's identity is partly defined by how a person's social entourage views him or her. Roy F. Baumeister, "The Self" in *The Handbook of Social Psychology*, 4th ed., ed. Daniel T. Gilbert, Susan T. Fiske, and Gardner Lindzey (New York: McGraw-Hill, 1998), 680–740.

16. Amy Cuddy, "Your Body Language Shapes Who You Are," TED talk, 2012, www.ted.com/talks/amy_cuddy_your_body_language_shapes_who_you_are.

17. Jennifer Petriglieri, "Under Threat: Responses to and the Consequences of Threats to Individual's Identities," *Academy of Management Review* 36, no. 4 (2011): 641–662.

18. Based on my interview with Cynthia Danaher after reading Carol Hymowitz, "How Cynthia Danaher Learned to Stop Sharing and Start Leading," *Wall Street Journal*, March 16, 1999.

19. See Rob Goffee and Gareth Jones, *Why Should Anyone Be Led by You? What It Takes to Be an Authentic Leader* (Boston: Harvard Business School Publishing, 2006), for a great discussion about managing distance and dilemmas of authenticity in general.

20. See Deborah H. Gruenfeld, "Power & Influence," video presentation, *Lean In* website, accessed August 27, 2014, http://leanin.org/education/power-influence/.

21. Charlotte Beers, *I'd Rather Be in Charge: A Legendary Business Leader's Roadmap for Achieving Pride, Power, and Joy at Work* (New York: Vanguard Press, 2012).

22. Charlotte Beers, "Charlotte Beers at 2012 MA Conference for Women," video, posted April 16, 2013, www.youtube.com/watch?v=VxjH0zYswzM/ The speech is based on her book, *I'd Rather Be in Charge: A Legendary Leader's Roadmap for Achieving Pride, Power and Joy at Work* (New York: Vanguard Press, 2012).

23. Susan M. Weinschenk, *How to Get People to Do Stuff: Master the Art and Science of Persuasion and Motivation* (Berkeley, CA: New Riders, 2013).

24. Bernhard M. Bass, *The Bass Handbook of Leadership: Theory, Research, and Managerial Applications* (New York: Free Press, 2008); Gary A. Yukl, *Leadership in Organizations* (Upper Saddle River, NJ: Prentice-Hall, 2010).

25. See Shelley E. Taylor, *Positive Illusions: Creative Self-Deception and the Healthy Mind* (New York: Basic Books, 1991).

26. The *Lake Wobegon effect* is the human tendency to overestimate one's achievements and capabilities in relation to others. It is named for the fictional town of Lake Wobegon from the radio series *A Prairie Home Companion*, where, according to Garrison Keillor, "all the women are strong, all the men are good looking, and all children are above average."

27. Thomas Gilovich, *How We Know What Isn't So: Fallibility of Human Reason in Everyday Life* (New York: Free Press, 1991): 77.

28. Jean-François Manzoni and Jean-Louis Barsoux, *The Set-Up-to-Fail Syndrome: How Good Managers Cause Great People to Fail* (Boston: Harvard Business School Publishing, 2002).

29. Roy F. Baumeister, Ellen Bratslavsky, Catrin Finkenhauer, and Kathleen D. Vohs, "Bad Is Stronger Than Good," *Review of General Psychology* 5, no. 4 (2001): 323–370.

30. People faced with unfamiliar role demands may have a harder time benefitting from negative feedback because they may lack the ability to assess independently the validly of the feedback they receive. As well, when people are insecure about their status, as neophytes are apt to be, they often adopt a defensive stance that reduces their ability to objectively assess negative information. Pino G. Audia and Edwin A. Locke, "Benefitting from negative feedback," *Human Resource Management Review* 13, (2003): 631–646.

31. Edgar H. Schein, "Kurt Lewin's Change Theory in the Field and in the Classroom: Notes Toward a Model of Managed Learning," *Systems Practice* 9, no. 1 (1996): 27–48.

32. Laura A. Liswood, *The Loudest Duck: Moving Beyond Diversity While Embracing Differences to Achieve Success at Work* (Hoboken, NJ: Wiley & Sons, 2009).

33. Erin Meyer, *The Culture Map: Breaking Through the Invisible Boundaries of Global Business* (New York: PublicAffairs, 2014); Fons Trompenaars and Charles Hampden-Turner, *Riding the Waves of Culture: Understanding Diversity in Global Business* (New York: McGraw-Hill, 1998), 83–86.

34. Rosabeth Moss Kanter, "Leadership in a Globalizing World," *Handbook of Leadership Theory and Practice*, ed. Nitin Nohria and Rakesh Khurana (Boston: Harvard Business Press, 2010).

35. For recent reviews of research on gender and behavioral expectations, see Herminia Ibarra, Robin Ely, and Deborah Kolb, "Women Rising: The Unseen Barriers," *Harvard Business Review* 91, no. 9 (2013): 60–66; and Robin Ely, Herminia Ibarra, and Deborah Kolb, "Taking Gender into Account: Theory and Design for Women's Leadership Development Programs," *Academy of Management Learning & Education* 10, no. 3 (2011): 474–493.

36. Anna Fels, *Necessary Dreams: Ambition in Women's Changing Lives* (New York: Pantheon, 2004).

37. Reid Hoffman and Ben Casnocha, *The Start-Up of You: Adapt to the Future, Invest in Yourself, and Transform Your Career* (New York: Crown Business, 2012).

38. The original definition of the term *identity work* comes from David A. Snow and Leon Anderson, "Identity Work Among the Homeless: The Verbal Construction and Avowal of Personal Identities," *American Journal of Sociology* 92, no. 6 (1987): 1336–1371.

39. See Herminia Ibarra, *Working Identity* (Boston: Harvard Business School Publishing, 2004), for a discussion of the difference between "plan and implement" and "experiment and learn."

40. Herminia Ibarra and Jennifer Petriglieri, "Identity Work and Play," *Journal of Organizational Change Management* 23, no. 1 (2010): 10–25.

41. Ibid.

42. Mihaly Csikszentmihalyi, *Flow: The Psychology of Optimal Experience* (New York: Harper Perennial, 1990); James G. March, "The Technology of Foolishness," in *Ambiguity and Choice in Organizations*, ed. James G. March and J. P. Olsen (Oslo, Norway: Universitetsforlaget, 1976).

43. Mary Ann Glynn, "Effects of Work and Play Task Labels on Information Processing, Judgments, and Motivation," *Journal of Applied Psychology* 79, no. 1 (1994): 34–45; and Leon Neyfakh, "What Playfulness Can Do for You," *Boston Globe*, July 20, 2014, www.bostonglobe.com/ideas/2014/07/19/what-playfulness-can-for-you/Cxd7Et4igTLkwpkUXSr3cO/story.html.

44. Researchers argue that work and play represent different ways of approaching, or frames for, activities rather than differences in the activities themselves. See, for example, Gregory Bateson, "A Theory of Play and Fantasy," *American Psychiatric Association, Psychiatric Research Reports* 2 (1955): 177–178; Stephen Miller, "Ends, Means, and Galumphing: Some Leitmotifs of Play," *American Anthropologist* 75, no. 1 (1973): 87–98.

45. Austin Kleon, *Steal Like an Artist: 10 Things Nobody Told You About Being Creative* (New York: Workman Publishing Company, 2012).

46. As cited in ibid.

47. Robert Kegan, Lisa Lahey and Andy Fleming, "Making Business Personal," *Harvard Business Review* 92, no. 4 (2004): 45–52. Christ Argyris further argued that executive's ability to learn shuts down precisely when they need it most due to their defensive reactions to avoid embarrassment or threat and avoid feeling vulnerable or incompetent. Chris Argyris, "Teaching Smart People How to Learn," *Harvard Business Review* 69, no. 3 (1991): 99–109.

48. Carol Dweck, *Mindset: The New Psychology of Success* (New York: Ballantine Books, 2007).

49. Salman Rushdie, "One Thousand Days in a Balloon," in *Imaginary Homelands: Essays and Criticism, 1981–1991*, ed. Salman Rushdie (New York/London: Penguin, 1992), 430–439. Psychologist Tim Wilson's research shows how much our narratives shape the ways in which we interpret what happens to us; changing the stories we tell about ourselves and our lives, even in small ways, is one of the most powerful tools for personal change; *Redirect: The Surprising New Science of Psychological Change* (New York: Little, Brown and Co., 2011).

50. Robert J. Thomas, *Crucibles of Leadership: How to Learn from Experience to Become a Great Leader* (Boston: Harvard Business School Publishing, 2008); Joseph L. Badaracco, *Jr., Defining Moments: When Managers Must Choose between Right and Right* (Boston: Harvard Business School Publishing, 1997).

51. Daniel C. Dennett, *Consciousness Explained* (Boston, MA: Little, Brown and Co., 1991).

52. Charlotte Beers, "Charlotte Beers at 2012 MA Conference for Women," video, posted April 16, 2013, www.youtube.com/watch?v=VxjH0zYswzM.

53. Dan McAdams, "Personality, Modernity, and the Storied Self: A Contemporary Framework for Studying Persons," *Psychological Inquiry* 7, no. 4 (1996): 295–321.

54. Herminia Ibarra and Kent Lineback, "What Is Your Story?" *Harvard Business Review* 83, no. 1 (2005): 64–71.

55. Hetain Patel and Yuyu Rau, "Who Am I? Think Again," TED talk, TEDGlobal 2013, June 2013, www.ted.com/talks/hetain_patel_who_am_i_think_again.

56. Bruce Lee, quoted in Bruce Thomas, *Bruce Lee: Fighting Spirit* (Berkeley, CA: Blue Snake Books, 1994), 44.

57. Bruce Lee's "Be like water" quote is as follows: "Be like water making its way through cracks . . . [A]djust to the object, and you shall find a way around or through it. If nothing within you stays rigid, outward things will disclose themselves . . . be formless. Shapeless, like water. If you put water into a cup, it becomes the cup. You put water into a bottle and it becomes the bottle. You put it in a teapot, it becomes the teapot. Now, water can flow or it can crash. Be water, my friend" (Bruce Lee, "Be Water [Longstreet]," video, posted December 26, 2012, http://youtu.be/bsavc5l9QR4?t=19s).

58. Kleon, *Steal Like an Artist*.

Chapter 5

1. "Lost enough to find yourself" (Robert Frost, "Directive").

2. George's story comes from Ruthanne Huising, "Becoming (and Being) a Change Agent: Personal Transformation and Organizational Change," paper presented at the annual meeting of the American Sociological Association, Montreal Convention Center, Montreal, Quebec, August 10, 2006.

3. Beginning with the end in mind was one of the seven habits in Stephen R. Covey, *The 7 Habits of Highly Effective People: Powerful Lessons in Personal Change* (New York: Free Press, 2004). The bestseller *Primal Leadership* also tells people to begin their change journey by identifying their "ideal self"; Daniel Goleman, Richard Boyatzis, and Annie McKee, *Primal Leadership* (Boston: Harvard Business School Publishing, 2002).

4. See Herminia Ibarra, *Working Identity* (Boston: Harvard Business School Publishing, 2004), for a description of the transition process. See also William Bridges, *Managing Transitions: Making the Most of Change* (Philadelphia: Da Capo Lifelong Books, 2009).

5. Laurence B. Mohr, *Explaining Organizational Behavior* (San Francisco: Jossey-Bass, 1982).

6. Edgar H. Schein, *Career Dynamics: Matching Individual and Organizational Needs* (Reading, MA: Addison-Wesley, 1978).

7. Alex Williams, "New Year, New You? Nice Try," *The New York Times*, January 1, 2009.

8. We only break a habit when we react to old cues with new routines that get us rewards similar to those we got with the old routines. Charles

Duhigg, *The Power of Habit: Why We Do What We Do in Life and Business* (New York: Random House, 2012).

9. For a great discussion of how this works with entrepreneurs, including himself, see Reid Hoffman and Ben Casnocha, "Plan to Adapt," in *The Start-Up of You: Adapt to the Future, Invest in Yourself, and Transform Your Career* (New York: Crown Business, 2012), 47–76.

10. For a great review of the latest thinking on goal setting, see Susan David, David Clutterbuck, and David Megginson, *Beyond Goals: Effective Strategies for Coaching and Mentoring* (Aldershot, UK: Gower Pub Co., 2013).

11. For more on the know-do-be of leadership development, see Scott Snook, Herminia Ibarra, and Laura Ramo, "Identity-Based Leader Development," in *Handbook of Leadership Theory and Practice*, ed. Nitin Nohria and Rakesh Khurana (Boston: Harvard Business Press, 2010), 657–678.

12. For a thorough discussion of the relationship between leader development and adult development, see David V. Day, Michelle M. Harrison, and Stanley M. Halpin, *An Integrative Approach to Leader Development: Connecting Adult Development, Identity, and Expertise* (New York: Routledge, 2008).

13. Most studies and people interviewed cited five to seven career changes in professional life. See, for example, "Seven Careers in a Lifetime? Think Twice, Researchers Say," *Wall Street Journal*, September 4, 2010.

14. See, for example, Gail Sheehy, *New Passages* (New York: Ballantine Books, 1996).

15. J. E. Marcia, "Development and Validation of Ego Identity Status," *Journal of Personality and Social Psychology* 3 (1966): 551–558.

16. Robert Kegan, *The Evolving Self: Problem and Process in Human Development* (Cambridge, MA: Harvard University Press, 1982). For a more accessible version of his theory, see Robert Kegan and Lisa Laskow Lahey, *Immunity to Change: How to Overcome It and Unlock the Potential in Yourself and Your Organization* (Boston: Harvard Business Press, 2009).

Conclusion

1. "Life . . . is really a search for our own identity," Charles B. Handy, *Myself and Other More Important Matters* (New York: Amacom Books, 2008).

2. Steve Jobs, Commencement address at Stanford University, June 12, 2005, http://news.stanford.edu/news/2005/june15/jobs-061505.html.

Index

Acknowledgments

This book has had a long gestation period, and I am especially grateful to those who gently pushed me to get on with it. I am particularly indebted to Melinda Merino, my editor at Harvard Business Review Press, and Carol Franco, my agent, for believing in this book, even in its "ugly first draft" form. Like the leaders whose stories appear within it, the book evolved through various phases, some smoother than others. Melinda and Carol encouraged me every step of the way, from my earliest ideas all the way to the finishing touches.

Melinda has been an amazing professional partner throughout the years. She encouraged me to consider how people learn to think like leaders and challenged me to move beyond my comfort zone in spelling out the practical implications of my ideas. She gave me space and confidence when I had to take a break from the project. She also showed remarkable patience when my perfectionism reared its head near the finish line.

Working with Carol has been a godsend. I've known Carol since we both joined Harvard Business School, but this is the first time we've worked together. Carol helped me "see" the book and craft the book proposal; she then struck an amazing balance between sharp professional advice and friendly motivational support. I'm also grateful to Carol for helping me create and deploy the extended network of people who bring out the best in a book. One of those people is Kent Lineback, who has taught me so much over the years about what matters and how to get it across in writing. Another gift from Carol is Mark Fortier, my publicist, who only just joined the team but has already provided much valuable coaching.

I have a great core team at INSEAD without which this book would still be a draft. Nana von Bernuth, my research associate and project manager, did more than I can ever describe to make the book come to life. Reaching far beyond her job description, Nana helped on all fronts, cajoling me to return to the book when it got pushed to a back burner, suggesting ways to make it more compelling and more applicable, and always giving prompt and valuable support no matter the time or place. Like the book's chameleons, she managed to morph her contributions into whatever I needed at each of the different stages of writing. I am especially indebted to her for her help with the second draft during the summer of 2014: I in Miami Beach, she on the Tuscan coast, both of us glued to our computer screens while our kids played in the sun. Although she had not considered writing one of her core strengths, Nana ended up giving me some of the most valuable editorial feedback I've had.

Another member of my core team I couldn't have done without is Mélanie Camenzind, my assistant for as long as I can remember. Mélanie kept everything organized and on track, taking all the distractions off my plate in her usual competent and professional manner. Expertly juggling my many diverse activities, she's made a do-it-yourself transition to a full-fledged project manager. Mélanie is a great example of how to redefine your job in order to make a bigger contribution.

Many friends and colleagues read early versions of my book proposal and chapters and listened to my ideas in seminars or in conversation. I am especially grateful to Gianpiero Petriglieri and José Luis Alvarez, whose insights into leadership have taught me so much, to Erin Meyer, who generously passed on everything she'd learned from publishing her book a year prior to mine, and to Kristen Lynas and Claudia Benassi, who were always ready to share their wisdom, bounce ideas around, and offer good cheer.

In more ways than I can enumerate, I relied on my Organizational Behavior colleagues at INSEAD at every step of this journey, from discussing classic studies in social psychology and organizational sociology to getting incisive feedback on title alternatives, book covers, and jacket copy. More often than not, they were willing to let me divert the lunchtime conversation to whatever I needed to mull over with trusted friends.

I had the good fortune and great pleasure to get to know Claudio Fernández-Aráoz in an earlier project on CEO performance. I am deeply grateful for his thoughtful and extensive feedback on the first draft of my manuscript and the many follow-up conversations that have guided me since. Claudio's area of expertise is development, and he practices what he preaches. I was a lucky beneficiary.

As my Leadership Transition faculty coconspirators, Gianpiero Petriglieri and José Luis Alvarez also played a crucial role in that long and iterative process of designing and delivering a course that fully addresses the needs of participants in transition to bigger leadership roles. A big part of the course's secret sauce is its stellar team of coaches, led by Martine Van den Poel, which helps participants personalize the learning and development process. I have learned a lot from their insights into the challenges executives face in the stepping-up process, and I'm grateful for their passion for helping people realize their potential.

The team at Harvard Business Review Press, including Dave Lievens, Lisa Burrell, Courtney Cashman, Sal Ashworth, Stephani Finks, Nina Nocciolino, Erica Truxler, Patty Boyd, Erin Brown, and James de Vries, has been amazing to work with. They are true pros and their work has made all the difference. I'd also like to thank Bronwyn Fryer, who helped me revise the manuscript after the reviewer feedback came in, making recommendations for clarity and style.

Books take time and resources to write. I've benefited enormously from the generous support provided by the Cora Chair of Leadership and Learning and the Patrick Cescau/Unilever Endowed Fund for Research in Leadership and Diversity. Not only did this endowment provide funding, it also brought me in touch with many folks from Unilever—Sandy Ogg (now at Blackstone), Jonathan Donner, Doug Baillie, Leena Nair, and Unilever CEO Paul Polman—from whom I learned much about what companies can do to help people step up.

And of course this book could not have become a reality without the men and women who generously shared their leadership transition experiences with me. This special group includes ten years' worth of Leadership Transition participants, my executive MBAs, and participants in my Deutsche Bank, Unilever, IWF, Siemens, and World Economic Forum Global Fellows leadership programs. While a few of them are featured in this book, many— from whom I learned just as much—are not. I deeply appreciate the lessons they taught me, and I value the confidence they placed in me by telling me their stories.

About the Author

Herminia Ibarra is the Cora Chaired Professor of Leadership and Learning and Professor of Organizational Behavior at INSEAD. An expert on professional careers and leadership development, Ibarra is the author of numerous articles on these topics published in *Harvard Business Review* and leading academic journals. Her bestselling book, *Working Identity: Unconventional Strategies for Reinventing Your Career* (Harvard Business School Publishing, 2003), is considered the premier reference on mid-career change.

At INSEAD, Ibarra is the founding director of The Leadership Transition, an executive program for managers moving into bigger leadership roles. She speaks and consults internationally on leadership development, talent management, and women's career advancement. She is a member of the World Economic Forum's Global Agenda Council and Chair of the Harvard Business School Visiting Committee. Thinkers50 ranked Ibarra number nine on its 2013 list of the fifty most influential business thinkers in the world. Prior to joining INSEAD, Ibarra served on the Harvard Business School faculty for thirteen years. She received her MA and PhD from Yale University, where she was a National Science Fellow.